PRAISE FOR *CHANGE*

"This is a book I wish I had written. Trautlein argues that leaders at all levels of an organization need to develop a strong Change Intelligence (CQ). Yes, yes, yes. Her model is easily understood. I can imagine leaders thinking about their own CQ as they read the book. The CQ Assessment should provoke good thinking and good conversation."

— *Rick Maurer, bestselling author of* Beyond the Wall of Resistance

"To succeed in the new economy, organizations must have the ability to identify disruptive innovation and the agility to stay ahead of the market curve. Leaders who understand their CQ are better equipped to facilitate open discussion and open communication, as well as empower their teams to recognize and act on opportunities more quickly. If you're looking for sustained growth and impact for your team or organization, *Change Intelligence* is a must-read!"

— *Charlene Li, author of the* New York Times *bestseller* Open Leadership *and founder of Altimeter Group*

"Trautlein's book provides a novel and compelling approach to change management that focuses on self-knowledge as the means for making effective change 'stick.' *Change Intelligence* invites change leaders to diagnose and understand their change management style and learn about its strengths and blind spots, all on the path toward building change intelligence. The book effectively identifies strategies for building our capacity to tap into the Head, Heart, and Hands of different change leadership styles. The book will be highly relevant and useful for any leader or manager trying to make effective change happen."

— *Jane E. Dutton, PhD, Robert L. Kahn Distinguished University Professor of Business Administration and Psychology, University of Michigan*

"As the president of a steelmaker in charge of leading changes from integrating acquisitions to pursuing new markets to implementing new technologies, I can tell you from direct experience that the CQ System works. *Change Intelligence* is more than just an entertaining read or abstract theory: Trautlein provides a clear roadmap for developing change leadership organization-wide using proven case studies on building bench strength from the executive suite to the shop floor and equipping change leaders."

— *Dick Teets, President and chief operating officer for Steel Operations and Executive Vice President for Steelmaking, Steel Dynamics.*

"*Change Intelligence* delivers the leadership Mojo you need to initiate winning streaks and to create profitable results for your organization."

—*Marshall Goldsmith, million-selling author of the bestsellers* What Got You Here Won't Get You There, Mojo, *and* Succession

"Technology today is evolving at an incredibly rapid pace, and leaders face daunting challenges implementing change in their organizations. Whether you're a CIO, IT project manager, or technology professional on the front lines, you'll find that Trautlein's *Change Intelligence* provides a practical, insightful roadmap to help you effectively engage and equip your teams to navigate toward successful and sustainable transformation."

—*Carolyn Leighton, CEO, chairwoman, and founder,* Women in Technology International

"Barbara has written a book that is both simple and complex. Through easy-to-understand language and examples, she explains the kind of thinking and actions a leader has to do to make change happen. Yet, she doesn't shy away from illuminating the complexities of change leadership. A very useful model for the twenty-first century."

—*Joel Barker, futurist and author of* Paradigms: The Business of Discovering the Future

"*Change Intelligence* offers an insightful, comprehensive analysis of what works and what doesn't in the change process. This book is packed with useful guidance for leaders at every organizational level who need to understand their own styles and roles in order to maximize their effectiveness."

—*Rosabeth Moss Kanter, Harvard Business School professor and author of* Confidence *and* SuperCorp

"*Change Intelligence* is an engaging read, enlightening for me personally as a leader and a great basis for team conversations. Understanding where you fall as a change leader is the compelling part of this book, and exploring the different styles of change leaders is incredibly thought provoking. Having gone through a sizable merger and facing system-wide change, the CQ process helps me as a CEO and my senior management team identify issues on how to lead our organization."

—*Peter Bergmann, president and CEO, Sisters of Charity Hospital, Catholic Health System*

"Getting change to be accepted and truly implemented remain two of the biggest challenges of management. Trautlein provides a simple and concrete triple-H framework (i.e., Head, Heart and Hand) that can help individual managers as well as teams and organizations ensure that they are addressing all relevant aspects of change. Not only does she present a useful framework, through her many concrete and real examples she shows how to apply the ideas in real life. The book provides opportunities for all of us, whether we are dominated by the Head, Heart or Hand, to improve our change intelligence."

—*Robert Hooijberg, PhD, Professor of Organizational Behavior at IMD, Switzerland*

"Cultivating talent capable of leading through change is mission critical. To execute a radical strategic transformation, we trained our 'leaders-at-all-levels' from the CEO to the Tellers and also our Board of Directors in CQ. Proactively building this enabling foundation equipped us to seamlessly serve members and emerge stronger culturally and financially from crises. *Change Intelligence* provides a practical approach, shared language, and a model to collaborate up, down, and across our organization."

—*Anita Countryman, SPHR, Vice President Member Experience, Rock Valley Credit Union*

"*Change Intelligence* not only provides a tool for identifying a person's strengths and blind spots for effective change, but also provides a practical 'how to use' guide through case studies. Walking through each scenario of high Heart, high Head, and high Hands articulates very well the watch outs that we all typically encounter and identifies what can be done to avert stepping on a landmine. Help the Hands, engage the Head, inspire the Heart; a winning formula for change execution."

—*Lyle Loutsch, Senior Director of Reliability and Engineering, Wells Enterprises, Inc.*

"Brilliant! Not only is Dr. Trautlein one of the most brilliant consultants I know, but she has the uncanny ability to take a very complex subject and design simple yet practical tools around it that lead to organizational success. A must read for any organization undergoing change!"

—*Linda Liang, PhD, President of Organizational Resources and Department Chair of the Doctoral Program in Organizational Leadership, The Chicago School of Professional Psychology*

"There must be more than a hundred books that have been written to help people cope with the changes that are imposed by external circumstances. However, there is another kind of change, where we attempt to alter the way we do things and the way our organizations function so that we can flourish when we are dealing with externally imposed changes. Dr. Trautlein's work identifies and describes the skills needed to effectuate change within an organization and provides individuals with the insights they need to develop their change leadership talents. These insights are practical and readily comprehensible because she recognizes that recommendations have to work on the shop floor and not just in the consultant's report."

—*Jeff Hazle, Senior Director at the American Fuel and Petrochemical Manufacturers Association*

"The one thing business leaders mess up most is the management of change. Too often they fail to strike the right balance between thought, action, and emotion, leaving their team—and themselves—confused and bruised. In *Change Intelligence* Barbara Trautlein rigs the game for you. This insightful, powerful book removes the mystique from effective change management and provides a intuitive but highly effective toolkit for managing change in any situation. Unless you spend your days working on your own in an underground bunker, you need to buy this book."

—*Les McKeown*, Wall Street Journal *bestselling author of* Predictable Success *and* The Synergist

"*Change Intelligence* is a well-articulated, well-grounded, and well-presented work on change leadership. The framework of change leadership and intelligence based on Head, Heart and Hands and the different change leadership styles is a fascinating one. It is a major contribution to theory as well as practice of change and leadership. It would be of use in diverse settings—both organizational as well as individual. The author motivates each of the styles with solid empirical examples, and develops them logically, coherently, and persuasively. The assessment tool that goes with this work will enhance the reach and the demand for this book. I have no hesitation in strongly endorsing this work."

—*Vipin Gupta, PhD, Professor and Codirector, Global Management Center, California State University at San Bernardino*

"Change is the work of leaders, and if you are going to do that work exceptionally, then the best place to learn how is in Barbara Trautlein's new book, *Change Intelligence*. She persuasively makes the case that the success of leaders now and in the future depends on their abilities to thrive on change, and *Change Intelligence* is full of the kinds of useful resources that will enable you to do just that. It offers extremely perceptive descriptions of the roles and styles of change, connects you to a highly useful self-assessment of your strengths and weaknesses, presents real-life case examples of change leaders in action, and contains dozens of practical tips and tools to improve your CQ. Change is hard work, but it'll be a lot easier after you've read and applied the lessons in *Change Intelligence*."

—*Jim Kouzes, coauthor of the bestselling* The Leadership Challenge *and Executive Fellow of Leadership, Leavey School of Business, Santa Clara University*

BARBARA A. TRAUTLEIN, PhD

CHANGE INTELLIGENCE

USE THE POWER OF CQ TO LEAD CHANGE THAT STICKS

RIVER GROVE
BOOKS

Published by River Grove Books
Austin, TX
www.rivergrovebooks.com

Distributed by River Grove Books

Design and composition by Greenleaf Book Group
Cover design by Greenleaf Book Group

Publisher's Cataloging-in-Publication data is available.

Paperback ISBN: 978-1-63299-724-1

Hardcover ISBN: 978-1-60832-442-2

eBook ISBN: 978-1-60832-443-9

Audiobok ISBN: 978-1-62634-606-2

First Edition

For my husband, Mike
Love, always

TABLE OF CONTENTS

AUTHOR'S NOTE

The core of each case study in this book is real. To preserve confidentiality, names and other potentially identifying details have been changed.

INTRODUCTION

Picture this: a $50 million steel mill—with a capacity to produce 1.4 million tons of steel per year—in bankruptcy. There I was, a twenty-five-year-old fresh out of college and on my first consulting assignment. I was standing in a room before two dozen steelworkers, all men, and all in their forties, fifties, and sixties. Almost to a man, they'd spent their entire career in the mill. It was my first day there, and I'd just finished introducing myself and explaining how we were going to transform the assembled group into high-performance, total-quality, self-managed teams. In the silence that followed my speech, a grizzled, six-foot-five, 250-pound steelworker stood up, stomped to the middle of the room, and declared, "We're steelworkers, and we don't listen to girls!"

What an illustrious start to my consulting career! The devil on my shoulder whispered a suggested response in my ear: *Well, maybe that's why you're in bankruptcy!* But the angel on my other shoulder won out, and I held my tongue.

Fast-forward two years. Despite that inauspicious beginning, we were able to work together to bring about a culture change that returned the mill to profitability—without a single layoff in the 750-person workforce. And we were able to do this in the mid-eighties, during a major economic recession.

Perhaps you're not facing bankruptcy like this steel mill, but I bet you'll answer yes to at least one of the following:

- Is your organization challenged in the current economy, forced to make tough business decisions that no one wants to make?
- Are you tired of the "program of the year" and want to know how to make change stick?
- Are you frustrated by your inability to overcome resistance to new ways of working?

If so, you're struggling with the process of organizational change, and this book is for you. As founder and principal of Change Catalysts, a change management consulting firm, I've had the privilege of working with such organizations as Abbott Laboratories, Ascension Healthcare, Blue Cross/Blue Shield, BP, Cisco, the National Institutes of Health, and Northwestern University. In my thirty-plus-year career, I've discovered that it is possible for change to result in bottom-line business benefits as well as empowerment for individual employees—if it is led effectively. And that's a big "if." So often, change is led ineffectively, without an understanding of how we can optimize ourselves to be the best change leaders possible. That's why I've developed my original, proprietary system for developing what I call "change intelligence," or CQ.

You probably know your IQ, your raw, intellectual intelligence—or at least the range your score likely falls within. You may even know your EQ, but if you don't, you've at least heard of the concept of emotional intelligence—your ability to understand and manage your own emotions and appreciate those of others to build more effective relationships.

But what about your CQ, your change intelligence? With all the dizzying, never-ending changes we are bombarded with, and all our frustrations with failed change, isn't CQ an idea whose time has come?

If you're a change leader—and we all are—read on. Whether you're a

CEO at a healthcare firm, a project manager who works in IT, or a sales representative for an engineering company, your workplace is buzzing with constant change. You need to know how to thrive in that change. You can't just tolerate change, like a leaf blowing around in the wind; you have to take charge of your career and your company and *lead* change.

The CQ System is a simple yet powerful model for change leadership. It includes (but is not limited to):

- an assessment to help you thoroughly understand your personal style of change leadership;
- a toolkit to leverage your strengths and bolster your weaker areas;
- coaching on how to mentor others through the change process;
- resources to help facilitate and launch new change teams, turn-around struggling teams, and build teams' collective change leadership capabilities;
- a global database of CQ research results, containing findings that are highly relevant for leading change around the world;
- a certification program to develop deep Change Intelligence and empower people to leverage CQ for the betterment of their organizations, teams, and careers.

In addition, you'll understand how you can integrate CQ with other potent change management strategies and tactics that you're already using to increase the probability that your change initiative will succeed.

This book is organized to help you understand what CQ is, how to diagnose and develop your own CQ, and then how to apply these strategies and tools to your teams, organizations, and beyond. The content is based on original research, relevant psychology and neuroscience, and grounded in solid methodology. I've included case studies from around the world, in dozens of industries and organizations to help you clearly understand how others have made CQ a reality. My goal is to enable you as a change leader to move beyond information to insights, beyond insights to action, and beyond actions to powerful results.

As is evident from the wide variety of cases in this book, CQ is relevant

- to individuals, teams, and organizations;
- from the C-suite to the front line;
- in industries as diverse as energy, healthcare, high tech, manufacturing, retail, and steel; and
- for changes ranging from mergers and acquisitions and new facility start-ups to new technology upgrades and new product launches, to new manufacturing processes and new human resource systems.

The chapters that make up part I provide an overview of CQ and introduce the CQ/Change Intelligence Assessment. Part II is all about you. You'll learn more about your specific change leader style and develop your own CQ, picking up tips, tools, and traps for each.

Part III takes a broader view, applying CQ to specific change situations. You'll learn how to intelligently lead teams through change and how CQ applies to organizations, exploring three firms in three different industries undergoing multiple significant changes at once. Finally, you'll see how CQ can be coupled with other change management tools and techniques at various stages of the change lifecycle (planning, doing, sustaining) and look at how CQ can help navigate the phases of human reactions to change (denial, resistance, exploration, and commitment).

Sprinkled throughout this book, you'll also find references to many more strategies and tools available on my website, www.ChangeCatalysts.com, to help you build CQ and start catalyzing powerful change in your career, team, and organization. In addition, you can download case studies on the "What is CQ" page, watch a sample video of my keynotes on the "Speaking" page, keep up with the latest CQ research on the "Resources" page, and learn more about CQ Certification on the "Certification" page.

PART I

CHANGE INTELLIGENCE:
WHAT IT IS AND WHY IT MATTERS

In Part I you'll learn what CQ is and why it matters—for your organization, team, and career. You'll explore the psychological and neurological bases for why we often struggle with change. Zeroing in on the unique change challenges experienced by leaders at different levels in the organizational hierarchy, you'll see how CQ operates in frontline, mid-management, and executive roles. Through learning the stories of real leaders facing major transformations, you'll see how developing change intelligence can help lead change that sticks.

Delving into the case studies will give you a sense of your own CQ and whether you tend to lead change with a focus on the "Heart" (people), "Head" (purpose), or "Hands" (process). You'll be invited to engage in self-reflection and observation, to diagnose your own CQ tendencies, strengths, and developmental needs. You will also obtain information about the CQ/ Change Intelligence Assessment, the tool you can use to determine which of the seven change leader styles best fits you.

CHAPTER 1

CQ: AN IDEA WHOSE TIME HAS COME!

Meet three change leaders.

- Glen is the CEO of a manufacturing plant that is the largest employer in a small Midwestern town. The plant's been shut down for two years, but it was just acquired by a new firm and is about to restart operations.

- James is a nursing supervisor in a hospital's intensive care unit, and he's embarking on an initiative that he hopes will improve the patient experience. At the same time, the healthcare system his hospital is a part of is going through considerable cost cutting and consolidation across its regional operations.

- Ann is the project manager in charge of a large-scale IT systems implementation for the sales team of her global consumer products firm. But the company has a strong history of resisting innovation; if it was "not invented here," most people aren't interested in using it.

What do each of these scenarios have in common? Major change is coming. What do each of these leaders have in common? They need to lead change effectively—for the benefit of their organization, their team, and their career.

When you hear the word *change,* is your first thought positive or negative? Are you filled with excitement and anticipation or with fear and loathing?

We often assume that because we're constantly bombarded with change in our professional and personal lives, we should know how to cope with it. We feel like we've been through so much change that we're used to it by now. We tell ourselves we can handle it, and we assume we can help others through most change processes. But from what I've seen, the reality is often quite the opposite.

Psychologists have conducted many studies showing that, almost all the time, our first reaction to change is to perceive it as a threat—something that causes apprehension, if not outright fear. It can be very difficult for most people to adopt the mindset that change can be positive, and that the new can be better, more enjoyable, and more attractive than the old.

As David Rock, one of the leaders in the emerging field of the neuroscience of leadership, and Jeffrey Schwartz, a leading researcher in neuroplasticity, note in their article "The Neuroscience of Leadership," "change equals pain: Organizational change is unexpectedly difficult because it provokes sensations of physiological discomfort . . . Try to change another person's behavior, even with the best possible justification, and he or she will experience discomfort. The brain sends out powerful messages that something is wrong, and the capacity for higher thought is decreased."[1]

As a leader, you are often called upon to lead change. How can you learn to approach change positively yourself, manage change so that it results in proactive benefits, and lead others to accept and even thrive in change?

Why Do We Still Struggle with Leading Change?

In the modern workplace, change is the only constant—an observation that is no less true because of its frequent repetition. Yet, as Rick Maurer points out in the latest edition of his book *Beyond the Wall of Resistance*, the failure rate of major changes in organizations has been alarmingly and consistently high since the mid-nineties.[2] In another study, researchers discovered that 86 percent of respondents "agreed that 'business transformation has become a central way of working.' [However,] the proportion who believe that business transformation is something at which their company excels ... is just 30 percent."[3] Every time one of these change projects fails, leaders and their teams get more discouraged, reducing the chances that the next project will succeed.

We're not talking about trifling changes, either. In a recent poll,[4] human resource professionals were asked, "What is the most significant change your organization will face in the next six months?" Here's the breakdown of their answers:

- Organizational restructure: 51 percent
- New leadership: 20 percent
- Acquisition/merger: 13 percent
- New product launch: 10 percent
- New technology: 6 percent

These are all large-scale changes that affect nearly every corner of an organization. Done right, they can enhance a company's performance dramatically; mishandled, they can turn into costly disasters.

So, while most companies today are highly experienced with change, they are far less experienced with change done right. Why is that? If your company is facing a major change and you've been asked to play a major role in it, you're probably wondering that too.

As it turns out, we know a lot about organizational transformation. For over two decades, authors have written hundreds of books on change management. We've developed multiple models for leading change, spanning from whole-systems approaches to methods like "preferred futuring" and "appreciative inquiry" to name but a few. We've conducted studies and found that positive change requires, among other things, a commitment from senior management, a "guiding coalition," and a "compelling vision." Experts emphasize the "burning platform": our workplace must be on fire before instinct kicks in and tells us to jump into the cold sea of change. We also know we have to answer the WIFM question— "What's in it for me?"—when persuading others to adopt a change. We've developed organizational-readiness assessments, leadership-alignment and stakeholder-engagement tools, and communication plans to help us through change.

With all this knowledge and all these methodologies, why do such a high number of major change initiatives fail? It's not that any of these models or tools are wrong or useless—they're just incomplete.

Successful transformations require more than book knowledge and theory, regardless of how sage and vetted the advice might be. To lead change, change leaders must know themselves. They must ask and be able to answer questions like these: What are my tendencies in leading change? What do I focus on, and what do I miss? What am I good at, and what can I get better at?

This powerful self-knowledge is the first step in developing change intelligence. And as leaders develop their own CQ, they begin to raise the CQ of their teams and the organization as a whole, dramatically increasing the probability of positive, pervasive change that sticks. Only when change leaders are equipped and empowered with this understanding of their personal working style can they guide others through transformation.

CQ: A Prehistory

In the early 1900s, Alfred Binet developed the first tool for understanding our own mental ability: the IQ test. Over the last century, many others developed cognitive tests and tools to help us understand everything from learning disabilities to our personal learning styles. By the 1980s, thanks to psychologist Howard Gardner, we'd begun to appreciate the existence of "multiple intelligences." Gardner helped us understand that people can be smart in different ways, beyond the traditional focus on raw intellectual intelligence. Some people excel in visual-spatial intelligence (artists, architects), others in body-kinesthetic intelligence (athletes, dancers), and still others in musical intelligence (composers, singers), to name but a few from Gardner's original list of intelligences.

Then, in the 1990s, emotional intelligence (EQ) came to the fore. Daniel Goleman popularized the term with his bestselling book, *Emotional Intelligence*, and created a model that demonstrated the importance of self-awareness and self-management, as well as social-awareness and relationship-management, in optimal functioning in life and work. Much research has been done on EQ, including the famous study at Bell Labs, which showed that EQ, not IQ, separated superior performers from average ones in the workplace.

Today, thanks to the work of Gardner, Goleman, and many others, we have a wide variety of self-assessments to help people evaluate and develop various aspects of their own "intelligences." We've seen an explosion in our understanding of how our minds, bodies, and emotions work together. Now, we're even finding provocative insights into our own behavior—including how our brains react to change—from neuroscience. David Rock and Jeffrey Schwartz write that "managers who understand the recent breakthroughs in cognitive science can lead and influence mindful change: organizational transformation that takes into account the physiological nature of the brain, and the ways in which it predisposes people to resist some forms of leadership and accept others."[5]

The CQ System

Change intelligence, or CQ, is the awareness of one's own change leadership style and the ability to adapt one's style to be optimally effective in leading change across a variety of situations. The idea behind the CQ System presented in this book is that each of us has a distinctive method of leading through organizational change. Just as we can measure our IQ, our EQ, and any number of our other intelligences, we can also assess our change intelligence. In doing so, we learn a great deal about how we can leverage our personal change leadership style to lead change far more effectively than before.

As noted earlier, it's not as if business leaders haven't acknowledged the importance of organizational change. We've developed ways to gauge the progress of a change project (such as change management audits) and methods for understanding the people impacted by change (e.g., *Who Moved My Cheese?*). But until now, there's been no assessment specifically designed to help change leaders understand themselves, even though this is the crucial starting point of any successful change initiative.

The CQ System I've developed enables change leaders to diagnose their change intelligence, equips them with applied developmental strategies, and shows them how to be powerful agents of transformation. I've spent the last two decades partnering with clients—from steel mills and sales teams, to refineries and retail, to healthcare and high tech—to lead organizational, team, and personal transformations. As a scientist-practitioner, I have conducted global change management research with leaders around the world and incorporated insights from psychology and neuroscience. All of that experience has gone into the creation of the CQ System.

During much of my early career, in the struggling plants of the Rust Belt, I facilitated various types of engagement processes, from self-managed teams and employee involvement to total quality management and lean manufacturing. More often than not, the senior management (and often joint union-management) teams I worked with thought I could come in, do a one-off soft-skills training event, and all of a sudden people would know how to work in a streamlined team environment, or make meaningful cost-saving suggestions, or conduct effective problem-solving sessions. I got in the habit of telling them I'd left my magic teamwork dust at home that day.

Just because we have mouths doesn't mean we know how to communicate. Just because we have brains doesn't mean we can solve problems. And just because we're social animals doesn't mean we know how to behave as productive, respectful members of a team.

Just a few years ago, when I was in India presenting at a conference on IT leadership and managing change, much of the conversation centered on frustrations IT professionals had as they tried to implement technology transformations. Their complaints ranged from business leaders "not getting it" and peer managers in other functional areas "not wanting it" to frontline employees "not using it." The mindset these comments revealed was interesting. These leaders saw change as something they did *to* others, not *with* or *for* them. They saw others as resisting change, when in reality, the "resisters" probably didn't understand the change, feel committed to it, or see its benefits. I wanted these leaders to turn the mirror back on themselves and see that the negative behaviors they saw in their teams were likely a reflection of a lack of effective change leadership on their own part.

Heart, Head, and Hands

The CQ System starts with the fact that each change leader has a basic tendency to lead with his or her Heart, Head, Hands, or some combination of the three. If you lead mainly from the Heart, you connect with people emotionally (I want it!). If you lead from the Head, you connect with people cognitively (I get it!). And if you lead from the Hands, you connect with people behaviorally (I can do it!). Depending on your natural inclination toward one of these, you have your own set of talents and areas to improve:

	Leads Change from the Heart	*Leads Change from the Head*	*Leads Change from the Hands*
Style	Engaging, caring, people-oriented	Strategic, futuristic, purpose-oriented	Efficient, tactical, process-oriented
Strength	Motivating and supportive coach	Inspirational and big picture visionary	Planful and systematic executer
Developmental Opportunities	May neglect to revisit overall change goals and not devote attention to the specific tactics of the change process	May leave others behind wanting to move sooner than people are ready for and lacking detailed planning and follow-through	May lose sight of the big picture and devalue team dynamics and individuals' emotions

It is not inherently better or worse to focus on the Heart or the Head or the Hands. However, the effectiveness of a change leadership style shifts in different scenarios depending on the type of change occurring, the business objective, the organizational culture, the people involved, and many other factors.

Of course, no one leads completely from the Heart, or Head, or Hands. Each of us is a blend of all three, and some people do lead with all three with equal savvy. But most of us tend to rely primarily on one or two of these aspects as we lead through change.

Many people are unaware of their dominant aspect (or aspects), and of the impact their leadership style has on the change initiatives they lead. But the effect of how you lead during change is significant—overreliance on the Heart, Head, or Hands to the detriment of the other aspects can alienate the people around you and limit your success. Fortunately, we can all build our capacity to use all three aspects and adapt our change leadership style to be more effective in any situation.

CQ in Action

To bring these concepts to life, I'm going to turn to the three change leaders I introduced at the beginning of this chapter. As you read, see if you can see yourself or others you know in the examples.

We'll start with Glen. When I worked with him, Glen was a manufacturing CEO who everyone respected for his turnaround abilities. The plant he led had been shut down for two years but had just been acquired by a new company. A few hundred members of the original workforce of several thousand were brought back to restart the facility. The revived facility was a "mini-mill," one of many that sprung up during the post-1980s renaissance of American steel.

Glen was a visionary. He was inspirational in communicating the future goals and big-picture business objectives. However, though he was really smart, he left his people behind. While he saw clearly in his own mind how to get from here to there, from decrepit and aged to high-tech and competitive, his people were confused. And that's what often happens—what seems like resistance is really confusion. His people thirsted for guidance because they did not want to be unemployed again, and the plant was the only game in town.

And that was the other thing Glen was blind to—the emotional needs of his people. There was so much fear. People had lost their jobs, and they desperately didn't want that to happen again. Yet when Glen demanded to know why things weren't happening fast enough, people would shut down, afraid to tell the emperor he had no clothes, that he'd never given them a plan or the training they needed to bring the vision to life.

Glen was stuck in his Head and needed to augment the Head with the Heart and Hands. I coached Glen on working through people's fears and giving them the skills to partner on the journey.

James, however, led with his Heart. A newly appointed nursing supervisor in a community-based hospital's intensive care unit, James was a highly respected and caring nurse, passionately committed to the hospital, his nursing staff, the physicians, and the patients. James spoke eloquently, sharing moving stories about serving patients and their families. He dreamed about overcoming the traditional silos dividing nursing, physicians, and administration.

However, while others were moved by his words and inspired by his passion, he was frustrated that no one seemed to be working with him to get from here to there. The administration seemed more focused on cost cutting, the physicians on building their own practices, and the nurses on resisting new cost-cutting programs and complaining about physician arrogance. Where was the team? Who was focusing on being of service to patients?

What James needed was to supplement his strong ability to focus on the Heart (to personally connect with people emotionally) with a focus on the Head (providing the business case that made financial sense) as well as the Hands (laying out a plan and delineating what it meant in specific, day-to-day behaviors). From our work together, James began to translate his motivating message into a plan and process that he could present to his manager and cascade through the ranks. While it's still a work in progress, at least there's a plan and a team of people beyond James working on it.

Ann—you guessed it—is a Hands person. Ann was an exceptional IT project manager who was given the opportunity to lead implementation of a new customer relationship management (CRM) system across her company's national sales organization. Ann brought a wide assortment of project management tools to her new assignment. She laid out a clever approach, consisting of a small team of highly trained CRM experts to rotate to each sales team around the country, spend a day training the sales professionals, and then go to the next. Sounds great on paper, doesn't it? Cost-effective, good use of resources, a leveraged plan. But it's this kind of thinking that brings to mind that old joke about consultants: Why are consultants like seagulls? Because they swoop in, eat your food, poop on you, and fly away—leaving a mess behind.

Though thorough planning is an important part of any great change effort, it's only part of the equation. Sure, Ann was savvy at providing people lots of tactical tools—a road map, milestones, time frames, and accountabilities. Yet people were totally unprepared for the change. They didn't know why the change was happening or how it was going to impact them. The company was a sales leader in their market, and they had always been told they were doing a great job with the tools they had, so people saw no competitive pressure to change. Clearly, my coaching with Ann focused on helping her move beyond a heavy-handed (or "Hand-heavy") change-by-checklist approach and to integrate the Head and Heart.

What can we draw from these three tales from the field? Each change leader had one of the ingredients but was missing the entire recipe for successful change. By adding the missing ingredients, they were able to overcome what looked like resistance but was really either confusion over the goal, lack of connection to the goal, or lack of training and tools to work toward the goal.

So many leaders are like Glen, James, and Ann. They keep doing things the same way, expecting a different result—the definition of insanity. We'd be better off taking the advice of the old Rodney Dangerfield joke: A man goes to the doctor in severe pain. He tells the doctor, "I've broken my arm in three places—what do I do?" The doctor replies, "Never go to those three places again!"

Change leaders often expect others to change, but they do not perceive the need to change themselves, or at least not their own change leadership style. As a psychologist, I know change starts with us as change leaders. And to lead change, we need all three tools in our tool bag: to start with the heart, engage the brain, and help the hands to get moving in positive, new directions. That's CQ.

Eisenhower said that leadership is "the art of getting people to do what you want done because they want to do it." Giving people the big-picture vision, the tactical plan, and the personal connection motivates others to move toward positive change.

Now let's revisit our three change leaders to see what happened down the road. In his words, Glen, Head-heavy CEO of the manufacturing plant, "got that the people stuff makes a difference." He made his leadership team partners in his own professional development as they were in the process of restarting the mill. Together, they invented systems and strategies not only for the technical side of the business, but also for the people side, ensuring two-way communication, a variety of engagement mechanisms, and training for people to be able to work together in challenging new ways. The start-up was described by the new parent company as the best of its over two hundred acquisitions. It exceeded all projections for quality, productivity, budget, and timeliness.

James, our Heart-driven nursing supervisor, is a work in progress. Through participating in a rapid action problem-solving team in his unit, he built an understanding of key business metrics and learned some tools for improving work processes. He is actively building his business acumen to connect himself and others to the "why" and "what" (Head), as well as his implementation skills to help the "how" (Hands), to augment his already moving, motivational messages about the "who" (Heart). As a high-potential leader, he reached out and is getting mentored by one of the hospital's administrative directors, who is recognized for her business savvy and ability to get things done.

Ann, the Hand-heavy consumer products IT project manager, was either unwilling or unable to adapt her behavior. After the first round of training for the CRM implementation, which resulted in low adoption rates of the new technology by sales representatives in the field, she asked to be transferred back to her previous role as an IT developer. She realized she didn't like the "fuzzy people problems" and wanted to work with people who were more "like her"—tactically oriented, focused on project deliverables—as opposed to dealing with what she perceived as the messiness of distracted business managers or uninterested end users and all their emotions, dynamics inherent in the job of a change leader.

Glen and James were not right and Ann was not wrong. Each grew in their self-awareness and made different choices for their careers, teams, and organizations. The goal of the CQ System is not to change people or force them to change, any more than change leaders can force change upon their people—at least not successfully, over the long term, without adverse consequences.

Instead, the CQ System offers a vista into one's own change intelligence and suggests how to adapt one's behavior to be more effective as a change leader when dealing with different people and different situations. It's not about changing who we are as people. It's about flexing our behavior to become more successful leading people through change.

As with any leadership competency, we need to have the will to build the skill. Learning that sticks, like change that sticks, needs to be self-initiated and self-directed. People need to have the opportunity to focus their attention on the goal and then to uncover their own insights along the journey.

Fortunately, we don't have to do it all alone. We can strengthen our less-used change muscles through consistent exercise. We can surround ourselves with others who excel in the areas we're weaker in. And we can get coaching on how to craft systems and structures to remind us to focus on those areas that are not typically on our radar screens.

Change at the individual level starts with awareness, moves to acceptance, and leads to action. The intent of this book is to help you become aware of your change leadership style, accept your strengths and weaknesses, and start to build your CQ to catalyze powerful change in your career, team, and organization.

In the next chapter, we'll explore the unique challenges faced by change leaders at different levels in an organization, and how CQ can help executives, project managers, and supervisors continue to learn and evolve as their influence and impact expands. In chapter 3, you'll learn how to diagnose your CQ, so you can begin to develop your change intelligence.

 Visit www.ChangeCatalysts.com/BookResources for a reading list that will help you further explore the topics mentioned in chapter 1, including change management theory and models, change management assessments and tools, relevant neuroscience research, and the concept of multiple intelligences.

CHAPTER 2

THREE LEVELS OF CHANGE CHALLENGES

As you saw in the tale of the three change leaders in the last chapter, change challenges vary by organizational level and role. For Glen, the manufacturing executive, the challenge was to restart the entire enterprise, transforming its traditional operating systems and organizational culture to be more competitive for the future. For James, the nursing supervisor, the challenge was to convince his boss to empower him to run his intensive care unit in a new way, and then convince his staff that the new way would be more empowering for all of them, including for the patients and families they serve. For Ann, the IT project manager, the challenge was to convince her team—made up of people over whom she had no formal authority—to adopt a new technology and a new business process.

So, not only do different types of change leaders face different problems, but their challenges are also impacted by where they sit in the organizational hierarchy. But no matter what position you currently fill, you will be able to lead change much more effectively when you understand how CQ works at different levels of your organization.

Even if they are "open" and participative, most organizations are still structured hierarchically. Change leaders can exist at any level of the hierarchy, but there are predictable differences in how people at the top, middle, and bottom relate to organizational change. Those at the top usually set the direction of the change and are most convinced of the need for it, but they tend to be isolated from many of the change's direct impacts. Employees at the bottom, though they are most removed from the rationale behind the change, are often most directly impacted by it; an alteration in their behavior is usually a significant part of the change initiative, and they can thus appear most resistant to it. Meanwhile, employees in the middle are squeezed between these two levels, sandwiched between the edicts of their bosses and pushback from their staff.

Case Study: Change Leaders at Three Different Levels

Frank was a newly promoted factory foreman in the steel mill led by Glen, the Head-focused CEO you met in chapter 1. As a supervisor, Frank was two layers below Glen, leading a team of three-dozen steelworkers in the melt shop. Melt shop workers are a unique breed: they labor in temperatures that reach 140 degrees Fahrenheit. When they start to melt the scrap, the light is blinding and the sound deafening. The melters' jobs are among the most dangerous and dirty in any industry.

The lead melters who reported to Frank each had more than twenty years' experience in the mill. Frank himself was one of the three youngest and most junior men in the melt shop. However, he had an excellent work ethic, and even though he got ribbed for having "gone over to the dark side" of management, his former peers gave him a break for having walked in their shoes.

Karen, a midcareer metallurgical engineer, was new to the industry and the mill. She'd been assigned as project manager of the continuous improvement (CI) initiative that was part of the recommissioning process. Unlike the large majority of her new coworkers, Karen wasn't around when the mill went bankrupt. She was unfamiliar with the town, the facility, and the people. She was seen as part of "Glen's gang," the new faction. People looked toward her with hope, but also with suspicion.

When the acquiring company appointed Glen CEO of the mill, there was a definite honeymoon period. Everyone was glad that they had jobs again and that the mill was bought out and restarted after two years of being shut down. Everyone loved the new, state-of-the-art equipment, but the changes Glen was making to procedures and policies—the way the people had worked for decades—felt like an affront. "We always tried to do a quality job with the tools we were given, didn't we?" they said in private. "It wasn't the way we worked that led us down the tubes. It was the economy!"

In Frank, Karen, and Glen, we have three change leaders at three different points in the hierarchy of the mill. Each faces a different set of obstacles. Although Frank didn't really "get" the changes Glen was asking—or rather, demanding—that he make, it was his job to "get 'er done" and start up a mill that boasted some of the world's largest scrap buckets and a capacity to melt more than three hundred tons of steel per batch. Although Karen certainly didn't "get" the people, the culture, or many things about how the place operated, it was her job to help install a culture of continuous improvement. And although Glen couldn't get it all done himself, he was accountable to the new parent company that had invested over $200 million in the facility—in a time of steep foreign competition in steel, demanding environmental regulations, and a down economy.

CQ for the Supervisor

As a supervisor, Frank is what I call the "bologna in the sandwich." He's caught in the middle, sandwiched between Glen, who wants to introduce new procedures, and his direct reports, who object to the procedures Glen's introducing. Sound familiar? Do you find yourself wedged in between the pronouncements of upper management (who are often far removed from the impact of the change on the organization) and your staff (who seem resistant to the change)?

Most new supervisors have much in common with Frank. Often, their first challenge in leading a change project is winning the respect of others—direct reports, peers, and managers. They are often expected to tear out of the gate and lead through a change process while balancing a very conflicting set of demands. For some new supervisors, this is their first opportunity to flex their change leadership muscles. Others, however, won a supervisory position because they've been informal change leaders all along.

Either way, how do you transition from being an exceptional individual contributor to being accountable for the behavior and results of others?

To survive as the bologna in the sandwich, you have to understand how your role as a leader differs from your role as an individual contributor. While you are dealing with these massive changes that come with your new position, be aware of the following demands you will experience as a leader.

As an individual contributor, you . . .	*As a supervisor, you . . .*
Are responsible for yourself	Are responsible for your team
Are measured by your own results	Are measured by your team's results

As an individual contributor, you . . .	As a supervisor, you . . .
Are focused on execution—you're a doer	Are focused on facilitating others' execution—you're a planner, a resource-provider, a barrier-remover
Receive feedback, training, and coaching	Provide feedback, training, and coaching
Deal with your boss and other employees, and perhaps customers and other departments	Deal up, down, across, inside, and outside the organization

In times of change, it is more important than ever for supervisors to model behaviors consistent with the transformation going on in the organization. What do employees want more than anything from their bosses? Time and again, surveys show they want their supervisors to walk the talk. Like many of his former peers, Frank hadn't always consistently performed his routine maintenance tasks or completed his associated data input duties on the shop floor. However, now that he was in management, with the maintenance supervisor as his peer, he understood that good record keeping had many benefits for the melt shop, spanning from tracking spending to conducting root cause analyses. As a leader, Frank knows that he has to embrace change, take responsibility for his team, and encourage them to take part in the changes that have come to the mill.

Ethan, one of Frank's melters, was one of the team members who struggled to consistently carry out the tasks he was supposed to. Ethan had experienced a fatality on his team early in his career, and he had driven to the employee's home and broken the news to the widow. The experience affected him deeply. He became a passionate advocate for safety. Frank helped Ethan make the very real connection between following standard operating practices and increasing the safety of the mill's operation. Armed with this insight, Ethan got on board with the change, and Frank got a powerful, well-respected partner to deliver the message to the troops.

Frank also showed his team how changing their behaviors cut down the costs for maintenance and the mill as a whole. This helped them draw a direct line between the changes they were being asked to make and why the changes mattered to the company.

Of course, as anyone who's ever tried to implement a new work procedure can attest, not everyone will buy in so easily. Frank realized that Joe, a very loud and intimidating guy who was an informal leader on one of the melt shop crews, was still not following procedure. Instead of berating and bird-dogging him, Frank observed and inquired. Thus Frank began to appreciate that Joe was intimidated by computers, and following procedures required entering data into the computer at the end of each shift. Recognizing the root of the problem, Frank worked with IT to simplify the computer interface, which—thanks to his own experience on the line—he knew was cumbersome anyway. Then Frank arranged for IT to retrain each crew on the streamlined process. Frank also coached some melters privately, one-on-one, and was able to boost Joe's competence and allow him to save face with his peers.

Getting the melt shop crews to follow the new procedures was just a small part of the recommissioning of the mill, but Frank had fired on all cylinders and gotten it done. As the bologna, he was squeezed in between Glen's mandate to follow standardized procedures, the maintenance supervisor's need for tracking data, and his crew's resistance. He overcame the resistance by

1. creating a trusting relationship between leader and team, and an emotional connection between people and the change;

2. providing information about the "why," thereby giving people the data they needed to make intelligent choices; and

3. removing barriers and providing the proper tools and training to know "how" to behave consistently with the change.

Said another way, Frank started with the Heart, then engaged the Brain, and then equipped the Hands. He built trust by acknowledging that he hadn't always followed procedure in the past. Then he gave people his reasons for not having done so—and explained why he was wrong.

Not all changes went so well for Frank. One challenge involved the implementation of a new type of scrap bucket. The buckets were purchased by the new parent company and were to be among the largest anywhere in the world. But crewmembers with dozens of years' experience in steelmaking expressed concern about the technical viability of the buckets.

Frank shared these concerns with his boss, Henry, the operations manager. Henry immediately dismissed the crew's concerns with the buckets. Instead of taking the opportunity to educate Frank, who could then have translated the message to the troops, Henry told Frank to tell the crew to focus on what they were supposed to do and leave the high-level decisions to those who knew what they were talking about. It was an old-school approach that didn't help Frank at all.

Frank wished Henry could see that, yes, his people were looking for information about how the scrap buckets were a sound business decision, but they also hoped to mollify their fears of a second shutdown. Henry was completely insensitive to the crew's fear that the start-up would be unsuccessful, the new parent company would withdraw its investment, and the mill would close once again.

What a missed opportunity! Frank was frustrated. His people's concerns were logical to him, and he didn't have the experience or information to rebut them. If only Henry, the operations manager, had made a few remarks at each crew meeting, it would have gone a long way. Henry could've had a partner in Frank, one who had the trust of the crews and excelled at communication where Henry clearly did not. Instead, he spawned another "mushroom"—kept in the dark, covered with dirt, and trampled on. (This incident unearthed not only Henry's blind spot, but also a clear developmental opportunity for Frank. He needed to learn how to "manage up," to influence those above him as well as he did those below and beside him.)

The new scrap buckets were installed successfully. However, the process to get there strained relationships and was much more painful than necessary.

Previously, as an individual contributor on the melt shop team, Frank used Heart, Head, and Hands to succeed. But after his promotion to supervisor, he was officially a change leader, and he had to use them in a new way. Here's what that transition looked like.

As an individual contributor, you . . .	*As a supervisor, you . . .*
Heart—Affective	
Treat others with respect	Engage and motivate others
Act as a good team member	Build a team
Head—Cognitive	
Understand the goals	Communicate the goals

As an individual contributor, you . . .	*As a supervisor, you . . .*
Learn the job	Train others
Hands—Behaviors	
Work the plan	Build the plan
Request resources	Provide resources

YOU, THE NEW SUPERVISOR

You may not be starting up a steel mill, but take a moment to consider just a few of the types of significant organizational changes a supervisor may be asked to lead:

- Implementing a new patient admittance process in a hospital emergency room.
- Installing electronic records keeping in a warehouse.
- Coaching call center representatives on a new customer service protocol.

In summary, here's an overview of the new supervisor as change leader, and some of the most common challenges you can expect to face in this role:

- You're often asked to lead change right out of the gate, even when you don't fully understand or support the change, and even when your people are resisting.
- Change initiatives are frequently communicated poorly from the top down, so you're often in a position of having to "inquire up" proactively so you can translate the message to the troops.
- It's incumbent upon you to position messages about the change initiative in a way that people can relate to. Your direct reports benefit from seeing the connection between what they're being asked to do

differently and why the change matters for themselves, their team, and their organization.

- You may need to play the role of buffer between your teams and the demands of others in the organization, particularly when change efforts are misguided.
- While you're usually not the originator of the change initiative, you're likely to be called upon to explain the "why" (Head) to your staff, to personify the Heart, and to be the Hands and execute the steps involved in the change. But you'll need help, so remember to provide the tools, training, and confidence that will enable people to make the change.

In *Communicating Change*, T. J. Larkin and Sandar Larkin describe the powerful impact of the frontline supervisor on the success of a change initiative. They state, and rightly so, that when changes are announced, most people do not look to the CEO for their cues, but to their immediate supervisor. What you—the supervisor—say and do makes a real difference.

CQ for the Project Manager

Karen, the metallurgical engineer we met earlier in the chapter, was a new project manager, charged with overseeing a continuous improvement (CI) initiative that was part of the recommissioning process. CI was a key aspect of Glen's vision for the new mill. He wanted to put systems and procedures in place so that the mill would restart successfully—and then stay that way in the long term. As he was fond of saying, "We're stretching people to do many new and different things, and we don't want the rubber band snapping back."

What are challenges unique to the PM role? We know that executives initiate change and supervisors implement them. Similar to executives, PMs can influence an initiative's overall direction, but typically they're not yet strategic leaders. Similar to supervisors, PMs are accountable for executing change, but they have to operate on a more tactical level as they plan and coordinate the change process, a process that typically involves people from multiple departments.

Here are some of the new and unique challenges faced by project managers, as compared to the challenges faced by supervisors.

As a supervisor, you . . .	*As a project manager, you . . .*
Are responsible for your team	Are responsible for your project team, which is most likely a temporary team whose members often report to other managers and who have additional and potentially conflicting responsibilities
Are measured by your team's results	Are measured by your project team's results, which are typically concrete and bounded deliverables; however, project scopes can also evolve over time (the dreaded "scope creep")
Focus on facilitating others' execution—you're a planner, a resource provider, a barrier remover	Focus on facilitating others' execution—you're a planner, a resource provider, a barrier remover; but you're often asked to use very specific, detailed, and complex project-planning tools to track budgets, actions, issues, and risks
Provide feedback, training, and coaching	Provide feedback and coaching, and acquire training resources if necessary
Deal up, down, across, inside, and outside the organization	Deal up, down, across, inside, and outside the organization; often compete for time and attention from project sponsors and other key stakeholders

Karen walked into constant chaos when she took on her role as lead for the CI initiative at the mill. As in most start-ups, people were stretched thin, pulled in a million directions, excited and stressed at the same time. In the midst of all this, Karen had to ramp up her new CI team quickly. They had to get to know their mission, their plan, and each other, but she was competing for scant time and attention—that of her team members, their bosses, and senior leaders.

Many people at the mill regarded CI as a long-term and fuzzy concept, and Karen wondered how she could possibly get this team to commit to the initiative, especially when she had no formal authority over them and they all had a plant to restart. At first she made lots of mistakes. People would miss her meetings and she'd have to scurry around the plant and round them up. When she reviewed the status of her members' assignments, nine times out of ten they hadn't been completed. Her status updates to her boss became increasingly embarrassing. After three months on the job, she'd made little tangible progress.

Soon Karen realized she absolutely had to turn around the sad state of affairs, but she wasn't sure how.

First, she apologized. She met with each of her eight team members one-on-one and admitted that she hadn't been sensitive enough to everything they had on their plates. She said she wanted to change that by getting to know each of them and understand their responsibilities. She asked them to educate her, and she listened as they talked. In this series of conversations, she built relationships, and she collected valuable data.

Second, she aligned with her team. After the individual meetings, she reconvened the team. This time, they all showed up as scheduled, and they were curious. She summarized what she'd heard in the individual meetings, which made every team member feel heard and understood. She acknowledged that CI seemed like a distant priority at a time when they were having daily challenges just getting equipment that hadn't been operated for two years restarted and getting new, complex technologies installed. "I know what you're all thinking," she said with a smile. "How can we continuously improve something when there's nothing to operate yet, let alone improve?"

With a few simple actions, Karen moved from being "against" her team to being "on their side." From doing something *to* them or *in spite of* them to rowing alongside them. Through listening and understanding their perspectives—what they were paying attention to—she saw a new way to focus their attention on the additional accountability of the CI initiative. She conveyed to them that, in fact, the CI process was a complement, not an impediment, to their other responsibilities. For example, Karen helped the supervisors on the team remember how difficult it was to get their people to adopt some new total quality management (TQM) procedures (a program initiated just before the old mill went bankrupt) because it was a change from how they'd always done things. How much easier would it be for the supervisors, she asked, to start right the first time? Moreover, she had them recall how in the TQM effort, an external engineering company had written all the procedures that the operators were supposed to adopt. How much more likely would people be to follow procedures they wrote themselves, while they were personally learning the best practices (and lots of bad practices through the mistakes they made as they progressed up the learning curve)?

In this way, Karen related the key components of the CI process to how the members of her project team would help the mill in the long term and how they would help the members of the team personally. The best time to start, she argued, is now.

In that first meeting of the rebooted project team, Karen worked with the members to craft ground rules for how they would work together in the future. She asked them for the best (or "least worst") time to schedule meetings, and was therefore able to improve attendance and ensure that tasks were completed on time. Importantly, she asked for permission in her role as team leader to conduct process checks when things were not progressing as agreed. In this way, by taking time to align upfront, the team owned the plan and process. Karen no longer felt like she was pushing on a string.

Karen supplemented these efforts within the team by aligning with key influencers outside the team. One of the members' biggest concerns was that while CI was a priority for Glen, it was not for their immediate managers. Karen took it upon herself to meet with each of their bosses to assess their commitment to their subordinates' active participation on the team. The engineering manager, who had two direct reports on the team, informed Karen brusquely that, "according to Glen, CI is our fourth priority, behind a safe, on-time, and on-budget start-up." An animated conversation about how a fourth priority remains a priority, not a non-priority, ensued. Karen tried to make the point that CI is a need-to-do, not a nice-to-do, a today-do, not a someday-do.

Clearly, she didn't have formal authority over the engineering manager—he was her boss's peer. Realizing the disconnect between Glen's mandate that CI is a business priority and the lack of specific tactics to make it happen, Karen set about systematizing. She crafted a project-planning methodology that listed all the major recommissioning strategies, including CI, and all the key activities to be accomplished for CI specifically. She shared that with her boss and asked for a meeting between the two of them and Glen.

In the meeting, she was able to demonstrate that if such a tool were used to guide not only her team's efforts but other strategic activities as well—and then reviewed at the weekly leadership team meetings—people throughout the mill would be jointly accountable to the same overarching strategies. With a common tool and language, conflicts between priorities could be proactively identified and addressed. Without criticizing or casting blame, Karen shared some of the struggles the supervisors and engineers on her team had as they tried to work on the CI project and complete their other tasks. She hinted that Glen taking an active role to encourage his managers to be jointly accountable for CI—as opposed to viewing it as a side initiative owned by Karen, the CI team, or the Quality department—would go far to stimulate progress.

Glen agreed to try out Karen's approach. It soon became a model for the rest of the mill, and it continued to be used after the mill was up and running. Her tool guided discussions about planning and the status of projects, from the leadership team to teams at all levels and in all departments. Thanks to this approach, people know the priorities of the company, understand the activities that support those priorities, and see the parts they are to play, and how and when they are to do so.

To achieve this success, Karen clearly had to be nurturing her change intelligence. Here's what the Heart, Head, and Hands of CQ look like as you transition from the supervisor to the project manager level.

As a supervisor, you . . .	As a project manager, you . . .
Heart—Affective	
Engage and motivate others	Engage and motivate others—who may only report to you part time, and over whom you may have no formal authority
Build a team	Build a cross-functional team—across disciplines you may not be expert in yourself

As a supervisor, you . . .	As a project manager, you . . .
Head—Cognitive	
Communicate goals	Communicate goals—not just to your project team members but also to their managers, departments, and down and up
Train others	Coach others through giving and receiving feedback; ensure they have the training they need to be effective project team members
Hands—Behaviors	
Build the plan	Build the plan, own the plan, and manage toward the plan relentlessly; resolve issues and mitigate risks through your ability to influence versus mandate
Provide resources	Provide resources—often through negotiating with other groups across and up the organization

YOU, THE PROJECT MANAGER

As Karen's story demonstrates, PMs need to balance relentlessly forging ahead with occasionally "going slow to go fast" by building relationships and enlisting partners. PMs must be flexible—they must know when to compromise, when to negotiate, when to stand firm.

Here is a summary of some of the typical change challenges you as a PM can expect to face:

- You need to be an expert communicator, not only within your project team but also up, down, and across the organization.

- As a PM, you need to develop sensitivity to agendas and political realities that may impact your project's success.
- Appreciating demands on your team members beyond their role on your team will help you strike a balance between supporting your members and getting the job done.
- Learning to link your project to other strategic objectives will help others prioritize appropriately and will allow you to get the resources you need, throughout the life of a project, even if you don't have free reign over the budget.
- Developing your ability to influence without authority, through a variety of means—from building trusting relationships to crafting plans with joint accountabilities—will go far to bolster your success as a PM.

Project management has evolved into its own discipline. A great many organizations now offer professional project-management certifications. Many of these programs focus heavily on the Hands—plans and structure—and promote a change-by-checklist mentality. It's not as if this information is incorrect; it's merely incomplete.

In the vast majority of cases, these programs offer little in the way of training on the Heart, the "people side" of change. Modules on change management are often cursory at best, rarely providing deep competence-building opportunities for emerging PMs.

And most of these programs do not deal adequately with the Head, either. They often encourage a focus on the goals of a project, but the vision for the change is often missed. Limited attention is given to the overall business strategy, and the pivotal task of helping others see the connection between their project and the big picture is downplayed.

PMs who are savvy enough to recognize the importance of the Heart, Head, and Hands, and who have the skill to incorporate all three into their repertoire, are much more likely to emerge as credible and successful leaders.

CQ for the Executive

Glen was born for the challenge presented by the recommissioning process. As a steel mill veteran of thirty-five years, he had a clear vision of how to take it from bankrupt and decrepit to profitable and world class. He and a small team of mill executives spent two years searching for a buyer of the mill's assets and negotiating with the new parent company. He knew the competition, he knew what new technology to purchase, and he knew the new operating practices to deploy to achieve his goal. He was an extremely strong, driven leader.

As an executive, Glen faced a different set of challenges than a project manager like Karen.

As a project manager, you . . .	*As an executive, you . . .*
Are responsible for your project team, which is most likely a temporary team whose members often report to other managers and who have additional and potentially conflicting responsibilities	Are responsible for the entire enterprise
Are measured by your project team's results, which are typically concrete and bounded deliverables; however, project scopes can also evolve over time (the dreaded "scope creep")	Are measured by success at the enterprise level

As a project manager, you . . .	*As an executive, you . . .*
Focus on facilitating others' execution—you're a planner, a resource-provider, a barrier remover; but you're often asked to use very specific, detailed, and complex project planning tools to track budgets, actions, issues, and risks	Are focused on creating vision and mission, setting strategy and plans, and enabling execution; balance the risk of standing still versus moving forward; own conflict between current systems and processes and those needed to support the change; clear the path for change
Provide feedback and coaching, and acquire training resources if necessary	Provide feedback, coaching, and mentoring, and enable systems for proper training, tools, and resources throughout the enterprise
Deal up, down, across, inside, and outside the organization; often compete for time and attention from project sponsors and other key stakeholders	Deal up, down, across, inside, and outside the organization; determine priorities for the enterprise

As a strong Head-oriented change leader, Glen had a clear vision for the future of the recommissioned mill. And as an engineer by training and an executive for decades, he knew the value of a solid plan to help the Hands achieve the vision. When Karen and the quality manager presented Karen's CI project plan to him, Glen realized he had slipped on that front. He had communicated a strategy but not helped people balance their priorities, resulting in misalignment and confusion. Making the time to meet with a frontline engineer gave Glen a dose of reality and helped him recognize that he had given an edict but not the guidance on how to bring it to life.

Given the nature of their responsibilities, executive change leaders can often be isolated from the impact their pronouncements have on the front line, and the barriers well-meaning employees face when attempting to enact them. Glen did understand, though, that "people stuff" makes a difference. Earlier in his career, while in one of his first managerial assignments, he had an experience that deeply changed his perspective as a leader. He had been leading a high-profile, multimillion-dollar shutdown, during which a galvanizing line was being updated with new technology. For the first time in his career, a project he was leading was not going well. The head manager from the construction firm took Glen aside and had a "come to Jesus" meeting with him. Glen could be pretty intimidating, and he didn't respond well to criticism, and the construction manager later said he felt like he was taking his own life—and the lifeblood of his company, given that this was an enormous project for them—in his hands.

The construction manager basically told Glen he was the problem—or more specifically, his leadership style. Glen ran every morning meeting like a "find the person to blame" session. People were afraid to say what was really going on regarding the status of the project, problems they were encountering, etc. If Glen banged his fist one more time on the conference room table, it was likely to explode into splinters.

At first Glen reacted defensively, but after taking a weekend to do some soul searching, he realized the guy might be right. While not one to apologize (or do anything else that might be perceived as a sign of weakness), Glen began to do things differently, using the construction manager as a kind of consigliere to give him feedback and advice about his style and how he could relate to people in new ways.

It's amazing how people can change when you change, and Glen found it out firsthand. He didn't alter his driven nature, but he did start listening more than he spoke, looking for contributions instead of people to blame, and asking rather than demanding. Although they were hesitant at first, over time Glen's people rose to the occasion, spoke candidly about the problems they were experiencing, and started to take on more accountability—the lack of which had frustrated Glen early on. While still over budget and late on delivery, the project ended up in a much better place than they'd feared it would prior to the intervention.

Glen was grateful the construction manager had spoken up, and he carried the memory of the rescued project throughout the rest of his career. Recognizing his blind spot, and cognizant of the need to keep people and their emotions on his radar screen, he invited our team to partner with him. He asked us to be the "keepers of the culture, the conscience of the steel mill." Working with Glen and his leadership team, we defined the vision for the new mill and turned lofty concepts—like continuous improvement and high-performance teams—from platitudes to specific behaviors that people could implement. We crafted plans for communicating the message and sharing strategies. Through our individual and group training and coaching with all levels of leaders at the mill, we heard firsthand stories of people's hopes and fears, and helped relay that feedback to Glen and his fellow executives so that they could proactively deal with them, thereby building relationships and trust.

Opening up the lines of communication alerted Glen to disconnects in his own organization and revealed how his behavior and the behavior of other leaders wasn't always supportive of the evolving culture. Glen worked with Henry to craft communications to help people understand the rationale behind the larger scrap buckets, and he partnered with the engineering manager to more appropriately prioritize the CI project. He navigated a line between talking to people directly and empowering managers and supervisors to deliver messages to employees. He thus created an atmosphere in which people knew him personally and could access him if needed, while also building the credibility of all the leaders below him and enabling them to build relationships and trust with their own teams.

Here's how Heart-, Head-, and Hands-driven change leadership in an executive differs from the same type of leadership in project managers.

As a project manager, you . . .	*As an executive, you . . .*
Heart—Affective	
Engage and motivate others—who may only report to you part time and over whom you may have no formal authority	Engage and inspire others—many of whom you have no or only limited and infrequent direct contact with
Build a cross-functional team—across disciplines you may not be expert in yourself	Build a cross-functional team with fellow executives, a staff team with your direct reports, and a feeling of teamwork and positive culture throughout the enterprise; ensure the organizational culture and structure are supportive of the new direction
Head—Cognitive	
Communicate the goals—not just to your project team members but also to their managers, departments, and down and up	Set the vision, goals, and strategy; communicate the goals; reinforce the goals
Coach others through giving and receiving feedback; ensure they have the training they need to be effective project team members	Coach and mentor others; ensure systems and processes are in place to develop people and manage performance

As a project manager, you . . .	*As an executive, you . . .*
Hands—Behaviors	
Build the plan, own the plan, and manage toward the plan relentlessly; resolve issues and mitigate risks through your ability to influence versus mandate	Build the plan, own the plan, and manage toward the plan; balance innovative tactics with risk management for the enterprise
Provide resources—often through negotiating with other groups across and up the organization	Acquire and approve resources for the enterprise; eradicate barriers that prevent people from thinking and acting in change-consistent ways

YOU, THE EXECUTIVE

Change at the enterprise level is by definition more complex, comprehensive, and challenging than any other. The buck stops with you. Here's a summary of what the executive change leader faces.

- While you have a vision of where you want to lead the organization, others may not see it as clearly. You have access to information about the external environment and overall organizational capacity that others may not. How can you direct attention so others can focus on what's important and better appreciate the new direction?
- Major transformation involves many changes at once. It's up to you to help align people on the right things and manage conflicting priorities and scarce resources.
- The higher you go, the less apt you are to get honest, accurate feedback about what's happening below you in the organization. How can you make sure you have adequate upward-feedback mechanisms?
- Be sure to evaluate systems and procedures to determine whether

they are supporting or inhibiting the change. Saddle a great change agent with a bad system, and the bad system will likely win out.

- Be visible and accessible during the change process, as much as is realistically possible. Actively champion change—and do not abdicate critical change tasks.
- Empower your managers and frontline leaders to deliver key messages. Arm them with as much information and support as you can.
- Be mindful of the impact of the changes on internal and external stakeholders, and on the overall organizational culture. Conduct frank discussions with fellow executives on the emerging dynamics, and speak up when a course correction is necessary.

Ah, strategy. Vision. Long-term horizons. Head-driven change leadership is the purview of executives.

Why did Larry Bossidy and Ram Charan feel compelled to write *Execution*? Because executives often drop out the "actually doing" part—the Hands.

And why the popularity of the TV show *Undercover Boss*? Because executives often fail to connect with the Heart; they're far removed from what their employees feel about any situation.

The most effective and well-respected executives, like strong leaders at all levels, combine Head, Heart, and Hands into their leadership style. And they remain engaged throughout the lifecycle of the change, avoiding the temptation to initiate and transition to the next new change challenge. The long-term success of any enterprise-wide transformation necessitates that executives play an active role throughout the duration by setting clear objectives and ensuring continued buy-in to the strategy. Visible, ongoing executive commitment is pivotal.

Leading enterprise-wide transformation can be the defining moment of your career. How you choose to lead that change will be a lasting part of your legacy.

 Visit www.ChangeCatalysts.com/BookResources for a reading list to help you deal with the unique dynamics faced by leaders at the supervisory, project management, and executive levels.

CHAPTER 3

WHAT'S YOUR CQ?

By now, you most likely have some idea of your own CQ. You've probably engaged in self-refection as you've read the stories of change leaders. You no doubt have a sense of whether you tend to lead with

- the Head—focusing on the big picture goal, the business objectives;
- the Heart—personally connecting with your people at an emotional level; or
- the Hands—providing teams tactical tools and skills like a savvy project manager.

And you've probably thought about what's missing from your change leadership style, too. One way to find out is to observe your people.

- Are they working really hard but misplacing their efforts? You may need to be more Head-oriented and paint a picture of the target and explain the *what* and *why* of the change.
- Are they unmotivated, indifferent, or even afraid? You may need

to add more Heart and share your own story, build trust, and show them that working together as a team benefits them and the rest of their peers.

- Or are your people paralyzed, like deer in the headlights, and can't seem to get unstuck and into effective action? If so, they may need a heavy dose of Hands, and you may need to set a plan, process, and skill-build to guide their efforts through the change.

Of course, none of us leads only, all the time, in every instance with the Head or Heart or Hands. We are each a blend of all three. It is this unique combination that represents our change leader style. When you've completed the CQ/Change Intelligence Assessment, you will have assigned yourself one of seven change leader styles: the Coach, the Visionary, the Executer, the Champion, the Driver, the Facilitator, or the Adapter. Each style indicates a different mix of Head, Heart, and Hands:

- If you're a Coach, you're all about Heart. You love engaging your colleagues whenever you get a chance, and you find great reward in supporting the people around you as you all move through a change process.

- If you're a Visionary, you are the one who's always looking forward to an inspiring future. Thanks to your Head focus, you have a gift for seeing opportunity and planning for new situations, and you tend to get excited about what lies on the other side of a change.

- If you're an Executer, you focus primarily on the Hands. You like to get things done, and people know they can rely on you to not just talk but take action. Often your execution is backed up by comprehensive, step-by-step plans.

- If you're a Champion, you use a combined strength in Head and

Heart to get people pumped about change. Like a Visionary, you see abundant possibilities for the future and, adding the people skills of a Coach to the mix, you're able to energize and excite your colleagues as you all work to bring about change.

- If you're a Driver, you're strong on both Head and Hands. You see an enticing vision before you, and you use your executional abilities to drive toward that vision, laying out clear strategies and tactics along the way.

- If you're a Facilitator, you focus on the specific people and specific activities you need to support on a day-to-day basis to lead the change, thanks to your strong Heart and Hands capabilities. You know the tasks that need to be accomplished to make measurable progress, and you succeed in motivating others to work together on those tasks.

- If you're an Adapter, you're about even on Head, Heart, and Hands. You can employ all three approaches as necessary, and you're generally flexible, politically savvy, and willing to collaborate with others. This may seem like the ideal style—and it does indeed have great benefits—but later on in the book you'll learn about some of the challenges Adapters face.

Figure 3.1 depicts the relationships between the seven change leader styles through their positions on a triangle (which, incidentally, is also the Greek symbol delta, which in science signifies change):

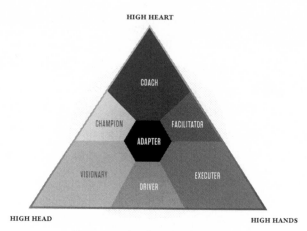

Figure 3.1: The Change Leader Styles

 You probably have a hunch about which style is yours, and you can find out for sure by taking the CQ/Change Intelligence Assessment, which you can learn more about at www.ChangeCatalysts.com/BookResources. Also follow that URL to view the CQ Triangle, which is the graphic representation of the seven change leader styles and their relationship to leading from the Heart, the Head, and the Hands.

The items that comprise the CQ/Change Intelligence Assessment represent key aspects of leading change, and the possible responses you're asked to choose from depict different approaches to them. The instrument was pilot tested with hundreds of individuals and in multiple client organizations spanning diverse industries. Change leaders comment that the instrument has a high degree of "face validity" (that is, the items "look like" what they are intended to measure) and that they can also validate their personal results (that is, the scores "sound like" themselves). Moreover, clients consistently report that their results are enlightening and actionable.

The CQ/Change Intelligence Assessment has been taken by thousands of change leaders from around the world. We now have a research database that enables us to understand how change is led globally. The database allows us to explore questions such as:

- What is the prevalence of the various Change Leader Styles, and how does this help us understand the success/failure rates of change?
- What is the dominant style of leading change in the C-suite versus on the front lines, and how does this suggest ways we can partner more effectively up and down organizations to achieve results?
- What if any differences exist across the globe, the genders and the generations, and how can these insights help us better understand each other's perspectives, value diverse contributions, and more positively engage for change?

These and other research findings are not only fascinating—they are also actionable. Keep in mind that it is also possible to analyze CQ/Change Intelligence Assessment results for your team and organization, which is a powerful, proactive, and strategic way to build collective change leadership capability and reach your change goals. I invite you to study the latest results, which are frequently updated as the database expands (visit the "Research" section of the "Resources" page at www.ChangeCatalysts.com).

What's Next?

We can all build our capacity to use all the aspects of change intelligence—our Heart, Head, and Hands. You'll learn more about your change leader style in Part II. Studying the chapter devoted to your style will provide you with targeted developmental strategies, which are immediately accessible, personally applicable, and professionally actionable, to hone your CQ to catalyze powerful change in your career, team, and organization.

 Visit www.ChangeCatalysts.com/BookResources for information about how to access the CQ/Change Intelligence Assessment and to download the CQ

Triangle graphic. Please note that you cannot navigate to the Book Resources page directly from the main www.ChangeCatalysts.com website; you need to type in the URL exactly as it is here (**www.ChangeCatalysts.com/ BookResources**) because it is a "hidden" page available only to book buyers. Once on the page, scroll down to "Chapter 3."

PART II

THE CHANGE LEADER STYLES

In Part II, you're going to dive deeper into each of the change leader styles. Whether you're a Coach, a Visionary, an Executer, a Champion, a Driver, a Facilitator, or an Adapter, there's a whole chapter for you. Reading the chapter closely will help you tremendously as you work to grow your change intelligence and understand the motivations of the people around you.

You'll look at case studies of real change leaders who demonstrated the mindset and behaviors of these leadership styles and zoom in on each style to see how it works in different parts of the hierarchy. You'll get a close look at a Coach executive, a Coach project manager, and a Coach supervisor; a Visionary executive, a Visionary project manager, and a Visionary supervisor; and so on. You'll explore the specific dynamics inherent in each of these combinations and delve into how you can capitalize on your strengths while shoring up your weak spots as your company, team, or career moves through major change.

CHAPTER 4

THE COACH

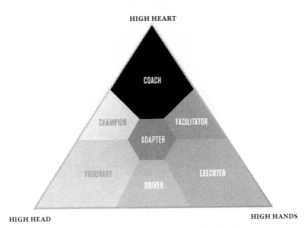

Figure 4.1: The CQ Triangle—The Coach

The Coach's Motto: To lead change, lead the people. Start with the heart.

Leaders with the Coach style of change leadership are defined by their orientation to people. They promote involvement, active listening, conflict resolution, consensus building, feedback, and an informal, relaxed climate. Generally, Coaches are considered positive people who, at times, seem to regard the process as an end in itself. The Coach may not confront other team members or give enough emphasis to completing tasks and making progress toward goals.

Get to Know Yourself as a Coach

As a Coach, you focus on people and how the change process will impact them more than any other type of change leader. You give significant time and attention to communicating about change, engaging others in the process, and ensuring that people's needs are taken into account as it occurs. You excel at encouragement, positivity, and support.

You may, however, place more emphasis on motivating people than you do on confronting them when they're not following through. To help yourself and others move more smoothly and deliberately toward the objectives of the change project, you need to find a way to supplement your natural people-focus with attention to project planning and the overall purpose and goals of the initiative.

Coaches in Action

The Coach case study takes place in a Silicon Valley telecommunications firm. Faced with rapidly advancing new technology, the dizzying flux of government regulations, and ever-increasing consumer expectations, this firm could be considered the epitome of change. The firm was relatively successful compared to its competitors, but its history was turbulent, characterized by frequent performance peaks and valleys. Executives and employees alike described their time at the company as chaotic and stressful, a roller-coaster ride. In part, the turbulence was attributed to lack of managerial consistency and executive discipline. Moreover, the firm experienced frequent turnover, particularly among women. As high-potential women approached the rank of senior manager, a large percentage left the firm.

Elizabeth's title was senior vice president of Workforce Innovation, and she was charged with transitioning the firm to a "culture of excellence"—no small task. High on her agenda was the problem of female turnover. First, Elizabeth instituted a variety of programs under the umbrella of "leadership development," including a three-day women's leadership retreat attended by the twenty-one most senior women in the firm—all those at director level and above.

When evaluations came in a week or so after the retreat, Elizabeth was pleased to see that the participants' feedback was highly favorable. The women said they had made connections across the firm; they reported learning valuable information, including tips on how to influence others; and they said they appreciated the access to more senior women in the company. Many of the participants described the retreat as "fun."

This was an impressive, encouraging reception, but what were the tangible outcomes of the program? Was the tide of turnover among high-potential women leaders stemmed, as Elizabeth had hoped?

No. In fact, it rose! In the months following the retreat, two of the twenty-one women leaders had epiphanies and decided to pursue other career interests. Through the discussions facilitated by the retreat coaches, the women had arrived at important insights into the company culture, such as its pervasive and blatant sexism, but when they got back to the office, they found themselves frustrated—they had no idea how to confront those responsible. Few revelations from the retreat had translated into concrete steps toward improvement.

But there was one tangible outcome of Elizabeth's retreat: it led to the development of a women's network within the company. While most of the firm's employees were located in the Silicon Valley headquarters, many were geographically dispersed across the United States, particularly those in sales and customer service. Jessica, director of the Midwestern regional office, was inspired by the retreat to create a virtual women's network, where women could support each other as they worked through the problems revealed at Elizabeth's retreat. She linked up with Sarah, director of the firm's Northwestern regional office, and together they got the job done.

Jessica and Sarah's women's network led to three mentor-mentee relationships between vice president– and director-level women and manager- and supervisor-level women. Within six months of its onset, the network helped one woman get promoted to head of a regional office, an opportunity she would have never known of or been considered for otherwise.

Another success story from the women's network was that of Kim, a newly promoted supervisor who was linked up with a director-level mentor through the program. Kim was excited about moving into her first formal leadership role, but she was intimidated at the same time. She'd been promoted through the ranks and now led a challenging team of customer service representatives, a group that experiences even higher turnover than the already high industry average, and which is also constantly asked to change how it operates due to frequently evolving service plans. But through her participation in the women's network, Kim gained valuable insights that enabled her to successfully transition from peer to boss.

ELIZABETH: THE COACH EXECUTIVE

Elizabeth was highly skilled at injecting energy and attention-grabbing elements into events. She used humor appropriately, even in highly charged emotional situations, and she enlivened meeting rooms with posters, collages, and other visual stimulants.

As company executives reviewed the feedback from the retreat, they felt Elizabeth's passion and commitment at a visceral level. Yet, the executives hadn't been presented with insights into how the women's frustrations impacted the firm's overall performance, or how to use the information derived from the retreat to help foster a culture of excellence (the task Elizabeth had been given). Considering the lack of concrete results from the rather expensive retreat, the executives asked Elizabeth to put her energies elsewhere as she sought to create the turnaround they were looking for.

What happened to Elizabeth after that? Well, she joined the ranks of company alumni and left the firm, eventually becoming the head of employee development at a nonprofit. She'd been able to engage a wide variety of women from across the firm, women at all levels and functions, but she was unable to leverage that effort to achieve bottom-line benefits for the company. Though she had connected with the women and made them feel heard through powerful—even soulful—discussions, she hadn't translated their very real and legitimate concerns into strategies that her fellow executives could buy into and execute.

Nevertheless, Elizabeth left a positive legacy at her former employer. Many of the women she worked with describe her as their personal mentor, a role she continues to fulfill for them today. She had sparked dialogue that resulted in the formation of the women's network, and she laid the foundation for the company's first leadership-development program for both women and men. "People development" and "reflection roundtables" are now part of the firm's practices. While her original task, the creation of a culture of excellence, remains a work in progress, the firm has become more consistently profitable and minimized the huge ascents and precipitous drops of the roller-coaster ride it was on before.

JESSICA: THE COACH PROJECT MANAGER

As a Coach like Elizabeth, Jessica loved every minute of the retreat, and the idea of a network for women leaders had originally been her brainchild. She felt somewhat isolated at her base in the outskirts of St. Louis and desperately wanted to keep the conversation going. Sarah, the Northwestern regional director who partnered with Jessica on the network, hadn't been as pumped as Jessica was right off the bat. Sarah was a strong Driver (we'll learn more about Drivers in chapter 8), and she initially rolled her eyes at Elizabeth's retreat idea.

However, Sarah quickly saw during the first day of the retreat that there was something to all this dialogue after all. At one session, she learned how her peers in another regional office handled a situation that had become a nagging problem for her staff. When Jessica reached out to her right after the retreat, she latched onto the idea of a women's network, which she saw as a way to continue learning actionable strategies for the unique technical challenges the firm faced. Jessica and Elizabeth, as Coaches, saw the people value; Sarah, the Driver, saw the business value. Sarah crafted the project plan for the women's network, and she and Jessica made the rest happen together.

KIM: THE COACH NEW SUPERVISOR

Kim, the employee who'd been newly promoted to supervise a challenging customer-service team, was matched with a director-level mentor as part of the women's network. Kim, too, was a Coach, and she had a knack for empathizing with the team (after all, they were very recently her peers). Kim understood their fears about potential outsourcing, their resentment over demanding workloads, and the frustration of constantly training new hires. When she interacted with her team, she wove stories about her own feelings and her own coping strategies into her communications. This enabled her team to genuinely connect with her and thereby connect with the job and each other.

However, Kim's relationship abilities also got in her way. She struggled in transitioning from friend to boss. This was the topic of several of her initial conversations with her mentor, who coached her to add more objectivity to her performance reviews and helped her conduct challenging—yet still caring—conversations that moved her direct reports toward positive change.

Kim knew how to coach positive behaviors and deliver positive feedback, but she also had to set clear, specific, behavioral expectations to give people constructive feedback when they were not performing to expectations, and to do so in a way that maintained the relationship while getting the job done. For Kim, this was doubly challenging. While she had always been a positive person, she wasn't always consistent about adhering to new customer service protocols herself. At times, she would make allowances for customers even though it was against policy, and several of her former peers knew this. From the vantage point of her new position, Kim had a bigger-picture view, and she saw the detrimental effects of this behavior. Becoming a supervisor was a challenging transition for Kim, as it is for many Coaches in their first leadership position.

The Coach's Strengths

Elizabeth, Jessica, Kim, and Coaches like them have the right idea—"start with the heart." These three Coaches understood what Jim Collins meant when he wrote about the importance of getting the *who* part right: "Most people assume that great bus drivers (read: business leaders) immediately start the journey by announcing to the people on the bus where they're going—by setting a new direction or by articulating a fresh corporate vision. In fact, leaders of companies that go from good to great start not with 'where' but with 'who.' "[6]

Elizabeth realized that due to internal turnover and external turbulence, most employees felt disconnected from the firm and its mission. She wisely avoided the Head-heavy approach right off the bat; she didn't focus on explaining the rationale and strategy behind the initiative. Nor did she launch into a Hands-heavy approach, cascading objectives and action plans down through the ranks to hold people accountable to rigorous performance targets.

Instead, she focused on the Heart, a Coach's specialty. She started by investing in people and their emotional connections to each other and the workplace. While facilitating discussions, Elizabeth frequently shared her own trials and tribulations, displaying vulnerability and building trust. She was consistently positive and often inspirational, conveying the possibilities she saw for the firm's future and encouraging the women to hone their leadership capacity for their own and the company's mutual benefit. Most important, she didn't just talk but actively listened, fostering a climate of open dialogue where people could explore meanings for themselves and give and receive feedback with their peers.

By starting with the affective and the emotional, Coaches lay the foundation for cognitive understanding and behavioral adaptation. That's a winning approach. Studies show that positive employees outperform negative employees in terms of productivity, sales, energy levels, turnover rates, and healthcare costs.[7] According to Shawn Achor, Harvard researcher and author of *The Happiness Advantage*, optimistic salespeople outperform their pessimistic counterparts by up to 37 percent. In fact, Achor shows the benefits of positivity across industries and job functions. For example, doctors with a positive mindset are 50 percent more accurate when making diagnoses than those with a negative mindset when they see patients.[8]

Heartfelt approaches like the ones Elizabeth implemented—roundtables, retreats, and so on—are winning ways to spark dialogue, encourage reflective learning, and create connections. They are great first steps in any change processes and great mechanisms to foster and maintain engagement along the way.

The Coach's Blind Spots

However, by themselves, these heartfelt approaches are incomplete. "Sharing sessions," a favorite of Coaches, can lead to even more frustration and cynicism when not augmented with a plan for action, as anyone who's attended a team-building event or two can attest. Women left Elizabeth's retreat inspired, but then they returned to their cubicles, received an invitation to attend a client lunch at Hooters or encountered some other demoralizing situation, and descended right back into dejection and anger. At *this* firm, dealing with *this* boss, in *this* client situation, what were they to do? How should they apply the heartfelt understanding from the retreat to their daily lives? They had no new systems to help them exert their power and make a difference at work.

While the connection between leadership development and fostering a culture of excellence made perfect sense to Elizabeth, her fellow executives didn't see the relationship as clearly. And when the invoice for the three-day women's retreat arrived—along with the letters of resignation from two top attendees—all of a sudden the executive team was paying attention.

Jessica fared better in her change project partly because she partnered with a different style of change leader. Sarah was able to help Jessica build the business case to convince the sales and customer-service executives to support the networking program, and Sarah also put the tactical plan together, showing how the logistics of the process would actually work (not typically a Heart-led Coach's strongpoint).

Similarly, Kim was wise to enlist a mentor to help balance her natural friendliness with formality and enforcement of rules, both of which are crucial to meeting challenging new objectives. Frank evaluations and discipline don't come easy to most Coaches, but Kim succeeded with help from a change leader who had talent in areas she needed to develop.

THE COACH AS A LEADER

Most of the time you . . .

- Encourage people to participate in discussions and decisions
- Step in to resolve process problems (e.g., conflict, lack of involvement)
- Listen attentively (while withholding judgment) to all viewpoints
- Recognize and praise others for their efforts
- Help the team reduce stress during challenging times in the change process by joking, being informal, and discussing personal interests

But sometimes you . . .

- See team process and organizational climate as an end in itself
- Fail to challenge or contradict others
- Do not recognize the importance of accomplishing tasks
- Overuse humor and other conflict-mitigating techniques
- Do not give enough emphasis to long-range thinking and planning

THE COACH AS VIEWED BY OTHERS

Usually people see you as . . .

- Encouraging
- Supportive
- Positive
- Tolerant
- Humorous

However, occasionally you are . . .

- Impractical
- Vague
- Not sufficiently serious
- Not bottom-line focused
- A pushover

The Coach on the Job

Let's now take a deeper dive and look at how Coaches at all levels—executive, project management, and supervisory—can capitalize on their strengths and work on their weak spots.

THE COACH AS AN EXECUTIVE

If you, like Elizabeth, are an executive and a Coach, you will often act as the conscience of your senior team. You'll keep people at the forefront and humanize the organization. However, because people occupy so much of your radar screen, you may not be as apt as your fellow executives to scan the horizon for new opportunities and important trends that will impact your business.

Strengths of the Coach Executive
- More than any other style of leader, you recognize the value of a participative organizational culture.
- You look for ways to promote engagement up, down, and across the organization.
- You want your fellow executives to be true change champions and to actively sponsor the change initiative.

- As part of the executive team, you model involvement and decision making through consensus. You devote time to engaging people on how they feel about the change effort.

Traps Coach Executives Should Avoid

- Do you prioritize people issues over tackling harsh business realities?
- When you talk about the benefits of change, do you express the benefits only in terms of the effect on the people, or do you also highlight the positive impact on the bottom line?
- Do you make the business case for your change initiatives? Have you positioned your ideas in a way that engages the Heart but also makes sense to the Head?
- Do you keep up with the business trends that impact your organization, enabling you to speak the language of your fellow executives?

THE COACH AS A PROJECT MANAGER

Jessica took on the task of co-creating a company-wide women's network, casting herself in the role of a midlevel project manager. As PMs, Coaches excel at creating a relaxed team climate in which every member feels valued and heard. However, PM Coaches are less likely to focus on the details of making change happen and may neglect project planning. This is why Jessica's partnership with Sarah, a determined Driver (see chapter 8), was so successful: each leveraged their own strengths and helped the other shore up their deficits, resulting in a powerful partnership.

Strengths of the Coach Project Manager

- You encourage participation of your team, even during the most stressful moments in the change process. When some team members are overly vocal, you ensure balance by bringing the more withdrawn members out of their shells.
- You ensure that interpersonal conflict on your team is acknowledged

and managed. You're good at setting ground rules for a healthy team atmosphere free of hostile competition, passive-aggression, and avoidance.

- You praise people for their efforts, and you take time to celebrate accomplishments with your team. Change projects can take months or years, and you more than any other style keep the benefits of periodic positive feedback and recognition front and center.

Traps Coach Project Managers Should Avoid

- Do you craft project plans with goals, action steps, deliverables, time frames, and accountabilities clearly delineated? Taking a hard look at how tasks fall through the cracks will help you as you work on more structured planning.
- Do you incorporate tangible metrics and concrete milestones into your change plans? For the Coach, such activities can be made more palatable by keeping in mind how achieving milestones are perfect opportunities for recognition and celebration, two of your strengths.
- Do you adequately monitor team members' work products and progress? Proper follow-up isn't the same as micromanaging. It's a winning opportunity not only to check in on a task but also to build relationships, offer support, and actively listen to the ideas and concerns of each team member.

THE COACH AS A SUPERVISOR

As a customer-service supervisor recently placed at the head of the team she'd worked on for years, Kim naturally empathized with those below her. Her team genuinely connected with her, too, and that helped them connect with their work and each other. But Kim had to learn how to not just coach positive behaviors but also to give people constructive feedback when they were not performing to changing expectations. If you are a Coach and a new supervisor, you may find similar challenges.

Strengths of the Coach New Supervisor

- You communicate well with the people you supervise and discuss change initiatives with them in an emotionally compelling way.
- You're good at tying change initiatives to something your people care about deeply.
- You usually know how people are feeling about the change initiative and can sense the mood on your team. You're supportive when people feel overwhelmed, stressed, or dejected. When people feel scared, you understand what they're afraid of losing—whether it's security, competence, or relationships—and find ways to alleviate their concerns in an honest and forthright manner.

Traps Coach New Supervisors Should Avoid

- Does your staff treat you more like one of the guys/girls than their leader? How can you transition from friend to boss?
- Do you shy away from giving constructive criticism because you think it might damage your relationship? How can you build the muscle needed to give difficult feedback to those who are standing in the way of positive change?
- Do your team members challenge you because you skirted the rules and didn't follow through consistently when you were their peer?

The Coach: The Bottom Line

When Coaches are at the forefront of a change initiative, people feel supported, inspired, and empowered. Steve Coats, a researcher on the subject of what makes a great leader, writes about the importance of this dynamic: "The responses we received through our research were both very interesting and consistent. For example, we noted how people almost always tended to respond based on how they felt, indicating 'I felt connected to my team members,' rather than 'There was a great deal of collaboration.' This should remind us all that the often cited quote, 'People may not remember what you say or do, but they do remember how you make them feel,' is certainly alive and well."[9]

Engagement through feeling is crucial. Jim Asplund and Nikki Blacksmith report on extensive research conducted by the Gallup organization, which has found that "employee engagement boosts organizational performance . . . We've also found that improving employee engagement links to improvements in crucial business outcomes (customer ratings, profitability, productivity, and quality) and reductions in others (safety incidents, shrinkage, and absenteeism)."[10] Clearly, Coaches, with their unending desire to connect with and involve the people around them, are not wasting their efforts.

It seems obvious to Coaches that "people issues" have a huge effect on the bottom line. However, they often stop short of making this connection for others. Coaches tend to deeply believe that engagement is an end in itself, which can lead to engagement taking precedent over performance. With no performance to show for their efforts, Coaches can come across looking less-than-effective as leaders.

What Coaches need to remember is that as change leaders, you need to make connections among people as well as connect them with the mission of the change project and the strategies that will get the job done. When Coaches strengthen their ability to do that, their power becomes significant. James Kouzes and Barry Posner, in their book *Encouraging the Heart*, describe what Heart-driven leadership is like when backed up with the specialties of some other change leader styles. Noting that the root of the word "encouragement" comes from *cor*, the Latin word for "heart," as does the word "courage," the authors observe that "encouraging the heart, then, is about the dichotomous nature of leadership. It's about toughness and tenderness. Guts and grace. Firmness and fairness. Fortitude and gratitude. Passion and compassion."[11]

There's no doubt that Coaches are crucial in times of change. They put people first, and they place a human face on every change effort they're involved in.

Self-assessment Questions

If you are a very high Heart change leader, ask yourself . . .

- Do you sometimes fail to engage in adequate project planning?
- Do tasks fall through the cracks because they have not been assigned or monitored?
- Do you tend not to make time to engage in scanning the horizon for new opportunities, trends that impact your business, or other entrepreneurial activities?

If you are a very low Heart change leader, ask yourself . . .

- Do you sometimes find that others are unengaged in the change process?
- Do people seldom come to you for coaching, to discuss problems, or to seek advice?
- Do people describe you as inspiring but not warm or caring? Do people see you as an effective task manager but not a leader of people?

 Visit www.ChangeCatalysts.com/BookResources for additional coaching hints on how Coaches can leverage their strengths and shore up their blind spots.

CHAPTER 5

THE VISIONARY

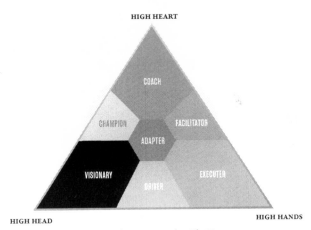

Figure 5.1: The CQ Triangle—The Visionary

The Visionary's Motto: Onward and upward toward new horizons! Another mountain to climb, another world to conquer!

The Visionary is a goal-directed leader who puts the vision, mission, and objectives of a change before all else. Most people see Visionaries as strategic, future-focused, big-picture leaders, interested in emerging trends and excited by new possibilities. But at the same time, Visionaries may not give enough attention to basic managerial tasks, and they may overlook the individual needs of others.

Get to Know Yourself as a Visionary

More than any other style, you focus on the long-term, overarching goals of the change process. You value the future and spend copious amounts of time and energy thinking about exciting new directions, scanning the horizon for what's next, and capitalizing on trends. You excel at independence, imagination, and forward motion.

In your zeal for new possibilities, you may, however, lose sight of current realities. You would do well to adopt a more tactical approach to the change process, focusing on delineating specific milestones, time frames, accountabilities, and resources to meet the objectives of the change project. You also tend to place too little emphasis on communicating with the people impacted by the change; thus, employees who work with or under you sometimes have unaddressed concerns and may not be fully on board with the project.

Visionaries in Action

Our Visionary case study takes place at a community-based healthcare system. Evan, senior vice president of Clinical Operations, had a penchant for proactively looking for new approaches to medicine. He actively networked with peers across the country, participated on boards, and scanned industry publications for new trends and best practices. At a conference for physician leaders, Evan attended a presentation by peers from another healthcare system and heard about how they had implemented a "corporate university" in their organization. After a visit to the facility, Evan became committed to bringing a similar program to life within his own healthcare system.

The timing was perfect. Evan's new program—the "Learning Center," he called it—would give employees training and development opportunities, and it would also be a testing ground for the new, innovative approaches Evan was introducing to the hospital. One such innovation he launched was Planetree®, a philosophy and set of practices that helps healthcare providers focus on patient-centered care in the face of budget deficits, regulatory pressures, staffing shortages, and metrics-based management. Planetree had already paid off in the form of a successful overhaul of the emergency department, and the vision was to extend that pilot success to other areas across the hospital.

Evan brought a project manager, Julia, onto his team to spearhead Planetree, among other initiatives, and he gave her the newly created title "director of quality." Julia was excited about her new role and the opportunity to further her vision of compassionate, high-quality patient care. She was thrilled her new boss shared her vision and had procured the resources she needed right off the bat to train a strong team and launch a pilot project. More than that, she was on cloud nine after the initial success of the emergency department pilot. She and her team had won accolades from department staff, nurses, and physicians.

Darrel, a nursing supervisor in the emergency room, was selected for Julia's Planetree team, which was comprised of frontline and midlevel staff from around the hospital who had demonstrated commitment to the idea of a patient-centered healthcare. He'd been instrumental in the success of the emergency department project.

The organization was thus focused on several forward-looking initiatives. Yet, these initiatives would all take time and cost money. Another faction at the healthcare system, led by Peter, senior vice president of finance, saw its financial situation as dire and in need of a much faster fix than programs like Evan's Learning Center could deliver. In Peter's mind, the root of the system's problems was inefficiency caused by people not being held accountable for the basics of their jobs. He thought the remedy was a rigorous process for managing employee performance.

Peter convinced the CEO that Evan's pet initiatives such as Planetree weren't working. The CEO then met with Evan and stated that he wanted to shift funds from the Learning Center to Peter's strategy of a new performance-management system. The CEO praised Evan for his innovative ideas but confessed that he'd been swayed by Peter's vision, which had been accompanied by a detailed plan, tangible deliverables, and financial payback. The CEO even hinted that he was disappointed with Planetree. Six months after an expensive new director—Julia—had been hired to launch the program, he was unaware of progress on the project.

During this meeting, Evan asked the CEO not to make a final decision on the spot, but instead to give him time to make the business case for the Learning Center. Based on Evan's track record and business savvy, the CEO agreed to meet with him again in two weeks to resolve the issue.

Evan immediately got to work. He contacted Julia and Darrel and asked them to collect the impressive tangible results of the emergency room pilot, which had increased patient experience, satisfaction, and bottom-line efficiency. He also asked them to come up with a list of problems they planned to tackle with the Learning Center, and how solving these problems would impact the hospital's metrics.

Armed with this information, Evan made his case two weeks later to the CEO, who was impressed enough to put the issue before the entire leadership team. In the end, two-thirds of the funds were given to the Learning Center, and one-third was given to Peter's performance-management system. A partial win—and a major lesson.

EVAN: THE VISIONARY EXECUTIVE

Evan started his career with this healthcare system as a practicing neurologist. He made a point of participating on and eventually leading various policy-making committees, and when the chief medical officer retired, Evan was asked to take the position. He actively lobbied for the title of senior vice president of Clinical Operations and for the expanded scope of responsibilities it implied. Evan aspired to interface between physicians and administrators, as would a traditional CMO, but he also had a clear vision of the future. He constantly thought about new directions in which his healthcare system could move.

Evan's passion for Planetree—and indeed all the new initiatives he championed—was palpable. He convinced the hospital's foundation to devote the proceeds from its largest annual fund-raiser to the Learning Center. But Evan was so distracted with his plans for the project that he didn't pick up on the behind-the-scenes wrangling of his peer in finance, Peter.

When Evan learned that the CEO was considering nixing the Learning Center, he was aghast. What did they think he'd been working on for six months? The numbers showed that the first Planetree pilot had been a demonstrated success. The Learning Center was poised to be another big achievement. It would house all the healthcare system's disparate, disjointed training and development events and form them into a comprehensive, integrated approach for building leaders. Why would the CEO pull the plug now?

It dawned on Evan that the CEO didn't appreciate the benefits that were around the corner because Evan hadn't helped him see his vision. Early on, Evan had persuaded the leadership team and the foundation to fund the Learning Center, but he hadn't kept them apprised of the project's progress. Evan himself had delegated responsibility for Planetree to Julia's team, and though he was aware of general progress, he wasn't sure of its current status.

While he'd been envisioning what lay ahead, his staff, his peers, and his boss had been moving in other directions.

After this realization, Evan partnered with Julia and her team to put together a business case that addressed the executive team's concerns—namely, the financial state of the hospital. Together, they broadened the business case to focus on other hard metrics (such as patient processing and wait times) as well as less tangible outcomes like employee engagement and quality of work life, both of which are critical to attracting and retaining physician and nursing talent.

JULIA: THE VISIONARY PROJECT MANAGER

To spearhead the Planetree project, Evan hired Julia to the newly created position of director of quality. Julia had been in the airline industry for fifteen years in various roles, including operations, customer care, and quality assurance. She'd earned her Lean Six Sigma Green Belt certification, an impressive credential for quality- and process-improvement professionals. Three years prior to joining the healthcare system, Julia's mother had been stricken with ovarian cancer. As her primary caregiver, Julia navigated the healthcare system for her mother, and although they'd received competent and kind care at times, she witnessed firsthand the many gaps in the treatment of patients and their families. After her mother succumbed to the illness, Julia became committed to transforming the healthcare industry, or at least a part of it she could influence. That commitment led to her career transition.

Julia built a strong team from across the hospital and hit a home run with her first project in the emergency department. She was living her dream, bringing her vision to life.

When Julia learned from Evan that the CEO was considering withdrawing his support for the Leaning Center and Planetree overall, it came as a shock. In working with Evan to present their impressive results to the leadership team, she realized how she had missed the opportunity to network and learn about the players and political landscape of the hospital. She neglected to strategically share the emergency room pilot success to ensure continued investment in Planetree's future.

DARREL: THE VISIONARY NEW SUPERVISOR

Darrel was frankly surprised at the positive feedback he received from his participation in the first Planetree project. As a proud nurse, he took his profession and its high purpose very seriously.

Like many of his fellow nurses, he'd been troubled by the administration's apparent placement of paperwork above patient care, and he saw Planetree as a way to right the balance. Darrel was satisfied to see that the administration was bringing the right people together to deal with what he saw as excessive paperwork that burdened nurses. He was thrilled that he'd been chosen as part of the team to take on the problem.

But Darrel's frustration with the old way of doing things was soon replaced by frustration with his fellow nurses. When, as part of the Planetree pilot, Darrel presented them with the changes to their emergency room procedures, they balked at the amount of paperwork (even though it had been greatly reduced) and pushed back on changes to their traditional work processes. The goals were clear—less paperwork, more efficient workflows—but Darrel struggled to obtain his team's compliance with the new procedures, much less their commitment to them.

Darrel, like many Visionary supervisors, needed to learn how to translate objectives into specific new behaviors for his team, and to work alongside the team as he trained them on their new roles. As it turned out, what looked like resistance among the nurses was actually confusion about what specifically to do. Darrel had initially stayed at ten thousand feet in his communications, and when he said "new and different," the nurses heard "more and difficult." Getting into the trenches with them helped Darrel explain the new streamlined, simplified tasks, to everyone's mutual benefit.

The Visionary's Strengths

Evan, Julia, Darrel, and Visionaries like them see the world as it could be, and ask, "Why not?" Evan hoped that Planetree would transform the healthcare system and help it achieve its mission. Similarly, Julia had a vision for improving the healthcare experience for patients and their families, so she switched industries, bringing her passion and years of experience to make it happen. Darrel shared a similar goal, to refocus clinical staff on their true purpose instead of on bureaucratic paperwork.

Ever seeking new opportunities, Visionaries seek out the new and different. They're drawn to novel ideas and to innovative ways to bring those ideas to life. Visionaries are usually quite inspirational as they communicate their hopes for the future.

Visionaries are both strategic and systems thinkers. Evan saw how the Learning Center could consolidate and advance developmental opportunities and accelerate leadership talent. Julia saw that her quality and customer-service skills were sorely needed by hospitals, and then made a bold career transition based on that insight. Darrel knew good record-keeping was important, but he saw how its overemphasis and poor implementation negatively affected the core functions of the emergency room. Visionaries see the big picture and the connections between the parts, and can help others see them as well.

The Visionary's Blind Spots

Visionaries' focus on the future can blind them to the realities of here and now. Caught up in his new project, Evan lost sight of new developments regarding the financial state of the hospital.

Beyond that, Evan lost focus on bringing the rest of the leadership team along with him on his journey. After he received funding, he was off and running. He missed several pivotal meetings of the leadership team and neglected to keep his boss informed.

By missing the human element, Evan lost support for his vision. And he missed critical information about what was going on in his immediate environment, as well as the competing priorities of his boss and peers. If he had remembered to engage with others, he would have obtained valuable cues about how to continue to link the Learning Center to important hospital priorities. In the end he did so, but almost too late.

Had Evan demonstrated to his peers that he had a solid plan that was moving forward, he would've ensured the continued confidence of the CEO, who had become wary of the expense when the hospital encountered financial difficulties. At the same time, Peter had advocated for a change in direction, denigrating the Learning Center as a pie-in-the-sky pet project of Evan's and describing it as a "nice to do" initiative at best. With no word from Evan on how the project was coming, it was no wonder the CEO became concerned and considered withdrawing his support.

While Visionaries motivate themselves with a zealous focus on the future, they often forget to share the tangible evidence of their progress, and the people around them lose sight of the purpose of the change initiative. The first Planetree project in the emergency department—a sector known throughout the hospital as a pit of animosity—was an undisputable success, acknowledged by staff, nurses, and physicians. Taking time to celebrate—and publicize—such milestone successes are critical when the change journey is long and major rewards not immediate. But because Evan wasn't in frequent communication with his staff and wasn't visible in the hospital due to frequent travel and offsite meetings, he missed this insight.

As did Julia, who was excited about her new position and the possibility of bringing to life her vision of reforming patient care. However, she was frustrated by how long it took her new colleagues—both on her cross-functional team as well as in the executive ranks—to "get it." Why didn't they immediately see the gold in what she was offering? The answer: because after Julia won her initial success, she was off to the next department, looking forward, but not around. Once Julia did connect herself to the people around her, she realized that networking energized her and fed her vision. Not only did she build valuable new relationships, but she also learned much more about Planetree opportunities throughout the hospital, which caused her to rework her project plan and position herself strategically for future leadership roles on other cross-functional initiatives.

Darrel was thrilled to participate on several forward-looking initiatives. However, he struggled to convince his staff to commit to the new direction; getting them to carry out their new day-to-day responsibilities was like pulling teeth. He needed to augment his compelling communications with specific, concrete training and tools that would help people do what they needed to do today, and address their very real concerns about the here and now.

Indeed, Visionaries can lose focus on the individual needs of others and on the organizational culture, its importance, and the impact of their changes on it. Fortunately, Evan, Julia, and Darrel had time to right their course. But had the CEO not given Evan a chance to come back down to earth before he lost funding for his various initiatives, the seed of positive, professional teamwork planted in the emergency department may never have taken root and spread into other areas in the hospital.

THE VISIONARY AS A LEADER

Most of the time you . . .

- Focus on the goal
- Look forward to the future
- Take a big-picture view
- Enjoy seeing new possibilities
- Scan the horizon for the next big opportunity

But sometimes you . . .

- Don't fully consider the effect a change will have on organizational culture
- May be less apt to focus on the individual needs of team members
- Complain about lack of progress toward goals
- Do not give sufficient attention to the process by which goals are reached
- Neglect to ensure that the tactical details of the change process are handled

THE VISIONARY AS VIEWED BY OTHERS

Usually people see you as . . .

- Forward looking
- Independent
- Imaginative
- A systems thinker
- A go-getter

However, occasionally you are . . .

- Too future oriented
- Not task focused
- Unrealistic
- Not concerned enough about team dynamics
- A bit of a dreamer

The Visionary on the Job

Let's now take a deeper dive and look at how Visionaries at all levels—executive, project management, and supervisory—can capitalize on their strengths and work on their weak spots.

THE VISIONARY AS AN EXECUTIVE

If you, like Evan, are a Visionary at the helm of an organization, you will perform the critical function of scouting out new opportunities, discovering trends that could impact the business, and steering toward brighter tomorrows. However, at times you may neglect the map and the needs of the people whose help you need to realize your vision.

Strengths of the Visionary Executive
- You're good at finding ways to capitalize on your love of casting a wide net for the new and different. You help your peers identify new directions and innovative approaches to achieving the goals of a change project.
- You encourage your organization to measure not only against past performance but against potential performance as well. You look at the opportunity cost of the decisions your organization makes.

- As a systems thinker, you help others see what is so obvious to you. You show them that the possibility is more than the sum of the parts, and you change people's perspectives. You recognize new synergies and connections that move the change initiative forward.

Traps Visionary Executives Should Avoid

- While you imagine new possibilities, are you keeping your feet firmly planted in the here and now? Are you focusing on the path you are proposing and on the people at your side?
- How can you translate your lofty vision to specific plans and tactical steps so others can confidently champion them?
- Have you communicated your vision for the change in a way that is simple, candid, and heartfelt? Do you discuss the vision, strategies, and goals for the change regularly in formal meetings and informal settings? Can the people affected by the change articulate the vision plainly and succinctly?
- What's the potential impact of your vision on the organizational culture? What's the current impact of the changes you have underway? What do you need to do differently to ensure an aligned and engaged workforce?

THE VISIONARY AS A PROJECT MANAGER

Julia was thrilled about the possibilities in her new position but frustrated by the pace of change and varying commitment level of her new colleagues. As a Visionary project manager, you have a chance to implement a specific vision while keeping your team members engaged and encouraging them to walk forward in lockstep with you.

Strengths of the Visionary Project Manager

- When your team gets bogged down in details and fails to see the forest for the trees, you motivate them with your inspirational vision of the future.
- Rarely satisfied with the status quo and often seeing beyond what's immediately present, you make your team smarter by facilitating discussions that encourage members to share their perspectives, educate others about their department and function, and brainstorm together for imaginative new ideas.
- You can usually envision the next project on the horizon after your current one is complete, and you're good at setting yourself up for success even before you get there.

Traps Visionary Project Managers Should Avoid

- Do you tend to become disenchanted with the details and the slow pace at which others adopt the change?
- Although it may not come naturally to you, as a PM you need to make a concerted effort to speak in a tactical language with your team. How can you produce and manage a detailed project plan that contains all the activities to get you from where you are to where you want to be?
- How can you make sure you're staying in tune with company politics and culture and coming to practical insights? How can you make sure you keep people issues and executional tactics on your radar screen?
- As a Visionary PM, you may be frustrated by your heavy involvement in tactical tasks rather than strategic planning. How can you use the opportunity of leading a project team—which may have members from diverse groups in the organization and sponsors in

powerful positions—to network, learn, and position yourself for new opportunities?

THE VISIONARY AS A NEW SUPERVISOR

As a Visionary new supervisor, you, like Darrel, may be enlivened by the possibility of playing a more strategic role but struggle to elicit the new day-to-day behaviors a change initiative requires of your staff.

Strengths of the Visionary New Supervisor

- You help your team see the "so what" behind the change. You're excited—and you make sure everyone else is, too!
- You communicate about the change in a way that helps your team see the connection between what they do on a day-to-day basis and the overall goal.
- When you are at your best, you leverage your skill in imagining new possibilities to understand why your staff may be resisting change, and you ask yourself how you can help them move forward.

Traps Visionary New Supervisors Should Avoid

- Have you communicated the expectations you have for your team members in very clear, specific, behavioral terms?
- Have you clarified your expectations—remembering that different words can mean different things to different people, and that some may need to see clear examples to really get what you're talking about?
- Have you confirmed your expectations by regularly following up, particularly in the initial stage of a change process, to make sure everyone is rowing in the same direction?

The Visionary: The Bottom Line

Visionaries provide an invaluable service to their organizations: they prepare everyone to meet the challenges of an increasingly uncertain future. A quote from futurist Joel Barker sums up the critical role of Visionaries well: "No one will thank you for taking care of the present if you have neglected the future."[12] Tony Mayo, a lecturer on organizational behavior at Harvard, has this to say: "The ability to visualize and articulate a possible future state for an organization or company has always been a vital component of successful leadership. In fact, when initially describing someone as a 'great business leader,' the knee-jerk reaction is often to cite something about his or her strategic ability or vision."[13]

But as we saw in our case study, balancing vision and execution is a Visionary's first key challenge. Mayo continues: "Just as important, [a successful leader must] possess the ability to oversee that vision's implementation." Visionaries must bring Heart and Hands into the equation, sharing their vision with others and laying out a path to the vision that incorporates many visible milestones along the way.

Remembering to bring others along is another of the Visionary's key challenges. In *The Leadership Challenge*, authors Kouzes and Posner list five Leadership Principles, and the first is "Inspire a Shared Vision." Visionary leaders can be inspirational, but they need to remember to inspire others as much as they get inspired themselves—the admonition is for a *shared* vision, after all.

Self-assessment Questions

If you are a very high Head change leader, ask yourself . . .

- Do you sometimes find yourself focusing too much on the future and neglecting day-to-day realities?
- Are you ever told that you have great ideas but lack systems and processes to bring them to life?
- Do you sometimes focus more on ideas than on the people who need to help implement them?
- Do you sometimes get frustrated that people don't seem to be following you in pursuit of the goal?

If you are a very low Head change leader, ask yourself . . .

- Do you sometimes fail to see the forest for the trees?
- Are you more efficient than effective—getting things done right but perhaps not getting the right things done?
- Do you at times miss the opportunity to capitalize on emerging trends because you are more focused on following through with an outmoded plan?
- Do you sometimes find yourself dealing more with internal team issues than with leading the team toward important objectives?
- Do your people seem uninspired?

 Visit www.ChangeCatalysts.com/BookResources for additional coaching hints on how Visionaries can leverage their strengths and shore up their blind spots.

CHAPTER 6

THE EXECUTER

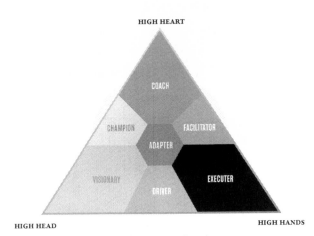

Figure 6.1: The CQ Triangle—The Executer

The Executer's Motto: Plan the work and work the plan.

Executers are, above all, task focused. They enjoy providing helpful technical information, and they make exceptional project managers. They do their homework, push others to set high performance standards, and use resources wisely. Most people see Executers as reliable, although at times they may get bogged down in details and data. Executers also neglect the big picture at times and are prone to overlooking the need for positive team dynamics.

Get to Know Yourself as an Executer

As an Executer, you're focused on the *process* of change. You pay attention to project planning, and you lay out the time frames and resources necessary to accomplish objectives during the change process. You're dependable, systematic, and efficient. Yet you may fall prey to a change-by-checklist approach, doing things "right" but not necessarily doing the right things. You may benefit from making time to look at the forest, not just the trees. You want to make sure you're working toward the end goal of a change project, not just hitting immediate tactical objectives. You'll also benefit from paying attention to the people along with the process, and making an effort to engage those around you.

Executers in Action

This case study takes place in a global pharmaceutical firm with multiple manufacturing facilities in eight countries. Even though the company was a market leader, the patent on its main product was set to expire in three years, which—given the dearth of promising new drugs in the R&D pipeline—would result in a significant drop in revenue. Company leaders had deliberated about a variety of ways to streamline and cut costs, and one of their strategies was to adopt a lean manufacturing philosophy in their production facilities. The lean approach would aim to enhance efficiency and reduce waste through a focus on engaging people in process improvements.

Simon, the company's senior vice president of global manufacturing, was selected as the lean initiative's executive sponsor. Allison, an IT professional with an operations background who had led a high-profile IT implementation in the company's U.S. headquarters, was selected as the project manager. Eight fellow high-potential young leaders from around the world were also chosen to work on Allison's team as "lean architects."

The firm also hired a global consulting company to assist the team in the initiative. Simon had worked with this consulting company in the past, and he'd seen firsthand why they had a reputation for fostering dependence in clients. He therefore mandated that the consultants work with the lean team only during the initial pilot phase of the lean initiative. They would help Allison's team develop the lean methods and tools, and the approach would be piloted at one facility. Thereafter, the lean team would be accountable for traveling around the world on its own and institutionalizing the lean process at each manufacturing facility.

The firm chose its Mexican manufacturing plant as the pilot site. The lean team laid out a plan of attack. The consultants conducted a "lean boot camp" for Simon, Allison, and the rest of the lean team. Following Simon's orders to codify the company's customized approach to lean manufacturing, Allison advocated creating a "lean playbook," a set of tools for planning, implementing, and sustaining the lean manufacturing approach at each of the firm's facilities. The lean playbook would lend structure and consistency to the team's global efforts.

Allison also laid out a well-planned approach to the pilot process. There would be pilots within the pilot plant, a series of "mini-transformations," so the team could have multiple learning opportunities within one facility, with different iterations and variations in approach. Allison thought this would be an efficient way for everyone to learn what worked best before they started implementing lean methods elsewhere.

After six months, results from the initial three mini-transformation projects at the Mexican plant were impressive. Supervisors and operators reported positive outcomes in their work lives, including the following:

- They and the workplace as a whole were more organized.
- More resources were devoted to the effectiveness of their work areas.
- They were reaching production targets originally thought to be unattainable.
- They were doing more than simply running and fixing machines; now they were thinking about how to solve problems and how to promote continuous improvement.

Yet, while the pilot participants reported "developing an eye for lean" and "building some lean muscle," all agreed it was too early to declare victory or to claim that "lean was baked into the DNA" (to use a few of the lean consulting firm's expressions). The mini-transformation projects had only involved three of the dozen production lines at the plant and had only tangentially involved supporting groups like maintenance, procurement, and shipping. And while the manufacturing manager was on board and heavily engaged—indeed, he was a self-proclaimed "lean zealot"—most of the rest of the plant's leadership team had only heard updates during their weekly meetings. Besides the initial boot camp, they hadn't been personally involved in the project.

Although the supervisors of the three mini-transformation lines had received lean training and participated on the projects, the process was heavily facilitated by the consultants, and much of the supporting data analysis was performed by Allison's lean team. On the participating lines,

production workers attended meetings and offered their ideas, helped organize and simplify their work areas, and collected data to track improvements, but they were far from running lean on their own. These three lines,
let alone the entire pilot facility, had a ways to go before they could be considered self-sufficient lean operations.

Opinions were mixed when it came to the Mexican plant's ability to
transition the initiative to its remaining production lines after the departure
of the lean architects and consultants. It would be a challenge for the line
managers to balance face-to-face coaching and facilitation with behind-
the-scenes data analysis and other activities. Some thought that it was too
much to expect a handful of lean-trained plant personnel to carry the torch
to other production lines—and then to the support functions—particularly in light of other initiatives occurring simultaneously at the plant.

Nevertheless, the expectations for the pilot had been met, so Simon
cleared the team to move to the main phase of the project: global implementation. He cited General Patton's rule: "A good plan executed today is
better than a perfect plan executed at some indefinite point in the future."
Allison proposed a SWAT-team approach, in which pairs of lean architects would rotate to each manufacturing site around the world, spend a
few weeks transforming the facility, and then go to the next. Simon quickly
approved the idea.

Allison was soon off to the company's largest manufacturing facility,
which was also the site of their corporate offices in the United States, with
a pair of lean architects. They met with the plant's leadership team and laid
out a plan for the mini-transformation schedule. The first rollout would be
in the chemical-processing area, which was led by Jack, a supervisor with a
background in chemical engineering.

Jack was pleased to be selected for the first mini-transformation at his
facility even though he'd only been with the company for six months.

During college, he had interned at other plants and had been exposed to the lean philosophy and other innovative manufacturing processes that were light years beyond what he considered the antiquated and inefficient systems at his current company.

Moreover, Jack resonated with the lean team's structured, well-planned approach to lean implementation. The mini-transformation rollout schedule seemed very logical, a good use of resources. The lean playbook provided methodical guidance for how to identify, plan, and execute lean opportunities on the production floor.

The process was kicked off at Jack's plant through another lean boot camp facilitated by Allison and her two lean architects. At the boot camp, Jack was surprised by the pushback he sensed—not only from his direct reports but also from the majority of the plant leaders.

At the Mexican facility, employees had a history of smoothly implementing new processes, and there was a culture of compliance with managerial directives. Not so at the U.S. plant: it had a history of resisting innovation and had a strong "not invented here" bias. The bulk of employees had worked at the facility their entire careers and had seen a lot of changes come and go, along with the young managers who spearheaded them. Their attitude could be summed up as "We'll outlive this program just like all the others. We'll just do our thing like we've always done. This too shall pass."

In Jack's mind, Allison and her team did as good a job as they could have. They worked through the agenda and the training exercises but were dogged by grueling rounds of questions and borderline hostile behavior from the plant's employees. Nevertheless, they were able to impart all the information they had intended to, and they provided examples of each tool in the lean playbook.

Soon the lean process was initiated in Jack's area. By the very next day, it had been abruptly halted. The plant's leadership had taken umbrage to what they heard in the boot camp and called a meeting with the company's global leadership team. They argued that Allison's team hadn't taken into account several important factors about how the plant functioned. These factors, they argued, would clash with the new lean practices. They further asserted that the transition to lean couldn't be accomplished with their "already lean" staff levels.

Several months of negotiations ensued. Simon personally met with the plant's leadership team and then repeated the exercise with the leadership teams at each manufacturing facility across the globe. He explained what lean is, what it would mean for the plant, and what needed to happen to get ready for it.

In the end, the lean process moved forward at the U.S. facility and at the other facilities around the world. Mini-transformations occurred in all of them and continued to occur for several years, albeit much more slowly and with more moderate results than anticipated.

SIMON: THE EXECUTER EXECUTIVE

In his previous job, Simon had seen the power of the lean philosophy and how it could lead to real results. But he was new to his current firm, and he hadn't taken the time to appreciate its history and cultural dynamics. He didn't travel to meet with them until the U.S. plant's leadership team stopped the implementation at its facility. It was the first time he had met many of them personally, and he soon apprehended that lean manufacturing practices were seen by some as contradictory to the company's traditional way of doing business. After a few discussions, he came to realize that adapting lean processes to the company's values, culture, and practices would be a challenging task. From the executive ranks to the shop floor, there were many different perceptions of how the lean approach could be integrated into the company's culture and core values.

Simon reengaged the global consulting company to help with the global implementation, and he encouraged them to facilitate frank, open dialogue among the executive team as well as among leaders at each of the manufacturing facilities. He hoped this dialogue would reconcile differing perspectives, generate working agreements, and give Allison's lean teams a better chance of reaching their goal. The meetings unearthed several factors that could potentially derail the mission, including lack of manpower, the highly variable skill levels of plant personnel, and inconsistent compensation programs that were seen by some as incompatible with lean principles.

Armed with knowledge of these issues, Simon was able to work with the right people to navigate around them and chart a new course for the lean project. With his expanded base of support, Simon could effectively communicate to the whole company that lean was a top priority. He was able to foster engagement by assessing the lean team's plans, progress, and results; he supported local site management as they balanced lean with other priorities, took risks, and made decisions that challenged people and processes; he devoted resources to the project; and he removed barriers to full implementation of the lean plan. As with any change initiative, the active involvement of an executive proved pivotal to success.

ALLISON: THE EXECUTER PROJECT MANAGER

Allison, an exceptional IT manager, brought all the tools in her tool bag to bear on her new assignment to oversee the lean transformation. She laid out a detailed plan with steps, activities, deadlines, and accountabilities for each member of the lean team. She led the development of the lean playbook, which served as a powerful foundation and reference for the lean team and each of the company's plants.

Yet there were certain dynamics that Allison missed as she led the team in taking lean worldwide. When the lean project was first launched at the Mexican plant, there had been much fanfare. For several months ahead of the launch, Simon and the plant manager had communicated with employees and prepared them for the coming change. At kickoff, there was an all-employee celebration. Updates on the initiative were given in team meetings, posters, and a wide variety of communication mechanisms.

Allison failed to appreciate how these efforts set the stage for the pilot. At the U.S. plant, her team engaged in sparse communication with employees. Allison's team met with the leadership team and expected that team to inform their staff, but Allison's team didn't give them anything specific to tell the staff, talking points or major topics to share. They provided some sample posters and emails to distribute about the lean approach and the success of the pilot in Mexico. But they didn't promote dialogue among employees involved in the pilot and employees at the other plants, and they didn't engage any plant personnel who weren't directly involved in the planning of the mini-transformations.

This lack of attention to the people-side of the process proved costly. Plant leaders didn't fully understand what they were getting into at first, and when they did, they balked. Conversations with their Mexican counterparts could have helped them understand what the lean approach entailed. It would've helped them set expectations and enabled them to proactively make changes that would support the lean implementation.

One of those changes should have been the creation of transitional organizational structures. Participants in the Mexican pilot had been eager to devote energy and resources to make lean work at their facility, so the lean team never fully appreciated how lean would alter roles and responsibilities. They didn't see that it would necessitate staffing changes when implemented at a much larger and complex facility.

The team's failure to actively engage staff members in two-way communication led to a rampant rumor mill. People heard "lean" and assumed it had something to do with downsizing and aggressive cost cutting. When the operators on Jack's team came to the lean boot camp, they were ready for war.

After lean implementation was put on hold at the U.S. plant, Allison and the lean architects took a step back to regroup and reflect. One of the lean architects was a Facilitator (described in chapter 9) and had questioned whether participants in the program had been given the resources they needed to be successful. Executers do provide training and tools, but at times they may fall prey to the flip-a-switch approach, believing that since they have conducted a workshop or demonstrated a new task once, people get it and can do it on their own.

The team began to consider abandoning its SWAT-team approach, or at least modifying it. They all recognized the need to create more robust lean teams at each manufacturing site. Just as the global consulting firm had mentored them and empowered them to conduct future lean transformations, so would the global lean team spawn a lean team at each site that would eventually take ownership of the initiative.

This would also enable the global lean team to have a better understanding of the cultural dynamics and historical work practices at each site. Thereby, while still adhering to their plan and playbook, they would have the insights necessary to make it a dynamic plan and site-customized playbook, further encouraging local commitment and bolstering the probability of sustainability.

JACK: THE EXECUTER NEW SUPERVISOR

Prior to the lean boot camp, Jack and his team were asked to collect data from their production line that would be used during the training process. Always one to do his homework, Jack decided on the greatest improvement opportunity, informed his team of his decision, and assigned each operator a specific set of data to collect.

During the boot camp, when they presented the data they had collected, Jack was disappointed by his team and surprised in the variability of their work product. So, after the training, when they began working on their first lean project, he kept tight control on the initiative, reminding his team members of their assignments during each huddle, checking in on each operator several times during a shift, and double-checking at the end of each work period.

After several shifts had passed, one of the lean architects—a Coach— asked to meet with Jack and review how he thought it was going. Jack said he thought the process was going well, that they were learning a lot about the root causes of their most nagging production problems and start- ing to see potential fixes. He thought the biggest issue was the operators' grumbling about their workloads now that they had new data-collection responsibilities.

The lean architect congratulated him on his progress and acknowledged the hard work he and his team had done. Then she shared some of the dif- ferences she noticed between the mini-transformation she'd facilitated in Mexico and the ones taking place on his line. Her chief observation was about the difference in the operators' level of motivation and positivity. In Mexico, operators were engaged and excited about having their voices heard and finally having an opportunity to make a positive difference in their workplace. On Jack's line, operators seemed to be more critical than committed.

Jack was a little defensive at first, but the Coach helped him see that his tendency to micromanage was taking all power out of his team mem- bers' hands. Instead of unleashing ideas and creativity, he was stifling them. *He* had become the barrier to innovation that he'd always hated! He saw that he'd expected too much of people who had never been exposed to lean before, and when they didn't live up to his expectation, he became far too controlling. Now his team felt oppressed and disengaged. Paradoxically, he had created the behaviors in his people that he most wanted to eradicate!

Structure can be empowering or disempowering. Systems can help people control their work process, or they can cause a feeling of being controlled. Enlightened with these insights from a caring Coach, Jack was able to reshape his relationship with his team. He went about securing their buy-in and gave them more flexibility to decide how to accomplish the team's goals.

The Executer's Strengths

Executers plan their work and work their plan. As Executers, Simon, Allison, and Jack were all systematic, efficient, and dependable. Simon saw the implementation of a lean manufacturing methodology as a way to achieve greater efficiency worldwide. Allison put her project-planning skills to use as she rolled out and systematized the lean initiative through mini-transformations and the lean playbook. Jack immediately embraced lean and put himself and his team to work in support of the project.

So often, firms focus on lofty visions and strategies—and nothing happens in the real world. Plans are put on paper, but nothing is implemented. Seemingly sexy strategies turn out to be all smoke and mirrors. Senior teams become enamored with their fancy retreats and high-priced gurus. Project teams get dewy-eyed with all the great work accomplished at their offsite session. Leaders at all levels get swept away by their latest, greatest revolutionary idea. But if there's no plan to execute, nothing will change. As Timothy Wilson writes in his book *Redirect*, "Research shows that people who focus on the *process* of achieving a desired outcome are more likely to achieve it than those who simply think about the outcome itself."[14]

This is where Executers shine. Executers provide comfort to their colleagues during times of change, because they demonstrate that there's a well-thought-out, realistic plan for accomplishing goals along the way. Executers establish practical strategies and make sure appropriate resources are devoted to initiatives. Indeed, what often looks like resistance on the surface is really fear or confusion; people simply don't know what to do or how to do it. Executers are great at helping others past this roadblock.

While other styles of change leader tend to gloss over the details, for Executers, tactical tasks are energizing, rewarding, and always at the top of the list. They derive comfort from predictability. In the face of instability, Executers excel at figuring out what to do to return to steady state, and what specific activities will make order out of chaos.

The Executer's Blind Spots

If only change were as simple as "plan the work and work the plan!" Executers can become surprised and frustrated that others do not follow through with their well-laid methods and procedures.

The SWAT-team approach sounded great on paper. But as they say, "Man plans, and God laughs." In the absence of empathetic, proactive, two-way communication about why lean was being implemented and how it would impact people, the rumor mill started and people resisted, setting the well-intended plan back months.

For his part, Jack made decisions and devised a plan of attack without involving his team. And he was insensitive to the impact of his change leadership style on how they were perceiving the lean initiative. He thought he was delegating, when in fact, he was disempowering, assigning his subordinates small tasks and not engaging them in meaningful work. Both Allison and Jack adopted a change-by-checklist approach.

Meanwhile, Simon convinced his fellow executives to adopt the process, sponsored a successful pilot, and felt confident handing off the future waves to his very efficient project manager, Allison, who clearly had a sound plan for execution. But he left out any consideration of the cultural, organizational, and political ramifications of the change. Focusing solely on execution, Simon lost sight of the big picture and all the many interconnections and interactions the change would impact. He planned for managing change, not leading change.

To help Simon out, the consulting firm educated him about the power of "personal change stories." Throughout history, humans have used stories to communicate, and during times of change, storytelling can be a powerful tool to engage and connect with people on an emotional level. Simon had learned a lot about lean processes at his former company, as had the participants in the Mexican pilot. They could have talked about how the change impacted the plant, its teams, and each individual. Yet, when he spoke about lean, Simon expressed himself in statistics.

Perhaps counterintuitively, stories are more compelling than statistics, and stories alone are more compelling than stories combined with statistics. Now that he understood that, Simon began incorporating his personal change stories about lean into his interactions with leadership teams at all the plants he visited. People got it. And they got it at an even more visceral, immediate level when Simon invited pilot participants to travel to plants that were just beginning their lean journey to share their stories. These pilot participants told of critical junctures where rapid decisions, risk taking, and leaps of faith resulted in turning around situations that had vexed their operations for years, sometimes decades. In this way, people could see how the change related to them and their everyday reality. After forging these personal connections, trust among people and commitment to the lean initiative increased exponentially.

THE EXECUTER AS A LEADER

Most of the time you . . .

- Excel at project planning and execution
- Accomplish your accountabilities in a timely and efficient manner
- Can be depended on to do what is asked of you
- Freely share all the information and materials you have and make sure others have the training, tools, and resources they need to perform their tasks
- Push the team to set high performance standards

But sometimes you . . .

- Lose sight of the big picture—the goal of the change process or the charter of the change team
- Lack patience with people and process issues
- Push for unrealistic performance standards
- Become impatient with other team members who do not live up to your standards
- Go into data overload, providing too much detailed information, writing reports that are too long, and offering long-winded explanations

THE EXECUTER AS VIEWED BY OTHERS

Usually people see you as . . .
• Dependable
• A planner
• Systematic
• Proficient
• Efficient
However, occasionally you are . . .
• Shortsighted
• Data bound
• A perfectionist
• Narrow
• Cautious

The Executer on the Job

Now, let's see how Executers work as executives, project managers, and supervisors.

THE EXECUTER AS AN EXECUTIVE

As an executive Executer, you grasp the need to continually keep the target on the radar screen for yourself, your team, and your peers.

Strengths of the Executer Executive

- You are a good counterbalance for your fellow executives, who may place a premium on vision while neglecting reality; who may value strategy over tactics. You utilize your practical, analytical mindset to ground the executive team.

- You tend to play devil's advocate to ensure that new visions and strategies are not simply a program of the year but instead are realistically achievable—even if they are a bit of a stretch.
- During stressful times of change, you ease tension by modeling reliability, dependability, and predictability, even in the face of chaos. You deploy systems and processes to make the change more controllable and therefore not so overwhelming.

Traps Executer Executives Should Avoid

- How can you minimize the risk of being pigeonholed as an implementer rather than an innovator? Are there ways you can challenge yourself to think and act more broadly?
- When you communicate about change, do you include facts and analysis as well as compelling stories and personal anecdotes? Do you include images along with the numbers?
- Are you bogged down in how things have always been done? Can you become involved in networking groups, where you might be exposed to how things are done outside your organization, or even your industry? How can you expose yourself to fresh, new thinking and outside-the-box ideas? Are you simultaneously managing for the present day, while keeping an eye out for new trends that will impact your organization in the future? How can you learn to take responsible risks?
- Is your organization efficient but not effective? Take time to periodically ask yourself whether you are not just doing things right, but also doing the right things. At times, particularly in complex or lengthy change projects, it's beneficial to take a time-out and revisit whether your change goals still make sense in light of evolving realities.

THE EXECUTER AS A PROJECT MANAGER

As an Executer, you're well suited to the role of project manager. You will, however, benefit from periodically stepping back to see the whole picture and asking fundamental questions about why you are engaging in certain tasks and what value they are truly adding, instead of simply checking the boxes diligently. Similarly, you would do well to involve others in such sense checks and to appreciate how others in your team and organization impact the success of your project.

Strengths of the Executer Project Manager

- You glory in the project manager role, deploying your natural talent for tactical planning and structured progress.
- You're good at providing your project team with resources, training, and tools required for success.
- You typically institute a regular process for managing actions, issues, and risks. Given your ability to create order out of chaos and to map out tactics to overcome obstacles, this comes naturally to you.
- You're good at focusing on nagging issues in the change process that you feel are out of control and establishing a rigorous and disciplined methodology to turn them around.

Traps Executer Project Managers Should Avoid

- Are you balancing execution with communicating the *why* of the change and *where* it's taking your team or organization? Do people focus on more than just today's to-do list? Do you take time to recognize significant accomplishments along the way? Some changes can take months and even years to achieve, so periodic celebrations, and even small pats on the back, keep people motivated.

- Are you bogged down in the details? The PM role is often a great opportunity to learn how other parts of the organization work. Raise your nose out of the tasks on your plate and get to know others and your organization.
- Toward this end, do you make it a practice to set up structured time to meet with key stakeholders and ensure that they're on board with the direction your project is headed? Although your plan may be logical and sound, if you haven't addressed the concerns of key stakeholders, they may not be supportive when the time for implementation comes.

THE EXECUTER AS A NEW SUPERVISOR

In transitioning to the role of supervisor, you will likely succeed where others struggle, particularly in planning and organizing work. But be mindful that you're not neglecting your team members. Seek to involve them in planning where it makes sense and engage them in dialogue about the direction of the change project at hand.

Strengths of the Executer New Supervisor

- You're talented at using your planning skills to create a logical system for making change happen.
- You help others be more organized by defining processes for your group to follow.
- You tend to set up regular mechanisms to monitor work and provide feedback, so tasks stay on track, course corrections can be made in a timely manner, and high expectations for output are met.

Traps Executer New Supervisors Should Avoid

- Do you keep people on the radar screen as much as you do tasks? Do you intentionally build time into your (usually rigid) agenda to check in with people, to see what they're doing and how they're feeling? Remember, people follow leaders who are competent but also caring.

- Are you sometimes disappointed by your team members' output? Have you assigned small, microlevel tasks instead of larger, more meaningful chunks of work? Have you assumed all the planning work for yourself, potentially stifling your team members' initiative and creativity?

- Are you overloading people? Expecting too much? Being too much of a perfectionist? You have high standards, and especially in times of change, people can get overloaded, need more time to perform at the right levels of quality and productivity, and may lose concentration. Do you know when to push and when to relax, at least temporarily?

The Executer: The Bottom Line

Instead of asking "Why?" or "Who?" the Executer's first question tends to be "How?" They get the vision and where they need to go, understand the current state of affairs, and see the need to plot an efficient course from here to there. They delineate who needs to do what, when, and how along the journey.

Executers have the right idea about the power of execution, but they need to expand their definition of the term. Larry Bossidy and Ram Charan describe execution as "the missing link, the main reason companies fall short of their promises, and the gap between what company leaders want to achieve and the ability of their organizations to deliver it." Yet, they define execution as "not simply tactics" but as the "way to link the three core processes of any business—the people process, the strategy, and the operating plan—together to get things done on time."[15]

In *Beyond the Wall of Resistance*, Rick Maurer describes the number one mistake leaders make that results in resistance to change: they "assume that understanding equals support and commitment . . . Making a compelling case for the change seems to be the biggest thing you can do to build support and commitment for a new initiative," Maurer continues, "and yet, it is the most overlooked task in the life of many changes."[16]

Remembering to incorporate the Head (vision and strategy) and the Heart (people and culture) would enable Executers to become more well-rounded and impactful leaders of change.

Self-assessment Questions

If you are a very high Hands change leader, ask yourself . . .

- Do you sometimes get accused of failing to see the forest for the trees?
- Do people describe you as an efficient project manager but not as a warm, caring leader?
- Do you find yourself more often being the implementer than the initiator of projects?
- Do you rarely schedule time in your calendar to look forward, consider new directions the company could take, or think creatively?
- Do people on your team seem to be completing their tasks without giving their all, thinking outside the box, or acting in the spirit of the change?

If you are a very low Hands change leader, ask yourself...

- Do your change projects veer off course, take longer than expected, or end up over budget?
- Do you sometimes neglect to take full account of actions, issues, and risks in the change process?
- Are you sometimes surprised at the status of projects and people's deliverables?
- Do you find yourself overwhelmed by all there is to do to make change happen and lacking a systematic approach to move forward?
- Do you get the feedback that people are inspired by you and like you, but do not see you as someone who effectively and efficiently gets the job done?

 Visit www.ChangeCatalysts.com/BookResources for additional coaching hints on how Executers can leverage their strengths and shore up their blind spots.

CHAPTER 7

THE CHAMPION

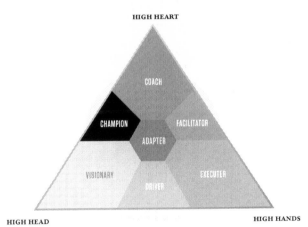

Figure 7.1: The CQ Triangle—The Champion

The Champion's Motto: Together we can make it happen.

Champions excel at rallying people around a change goal. They value engaging with a wide variety of people and inspiring them toward exciting new possibilities. People see Champions as compelling, charismatic, and enlightening.

Get to Know Yourself as a Champion

Some people refer to Champions as "participative visionaries" because of their emphasis on long-term goals combined with their ability to get others involved in developing and implementing those goals. As a Champion, you demonstrate considerable skill in rallying people in support of the new and the different. However, you may at times not give sufficient attention to the immediate task or the short-term objectives of a change project. Since you are more apt to promote the positive aspects of the change, you may not invite and pay sufficient attention to constructive criticism about the goals and the process.

As a Champion, you are verbally adept and persuasive, but some may see you as insincere or manipulative. Others may wonder whether your natural effusiveness is a cover for other intentions, and whether you are excited about the greater good or are really out for yourself. You must therefore be sensitive to how you come across so as not to appear calculating and insufficiently grounded; people may otherwise see you as disconnected from the reality of the current situation and out of sync with the specific tactics necessary to reaching a goal. Tempering enthusiasm and grand visions with detailed plans and objectives will enable you to influence those who are technically oriented or more focused on the business process.

Champions in Action

This case study focuses on a significant IT project inside a large utility company. The purpose of the project was to implement an information management (IM) system consisting of new technologies and new organizational processes. The utility had grown by acquisition and therefore had a multitude of legacy systems, resulting in each of its four business units and the corporate offices using different technologies and following different information management protocols. It was a complicated arrangement that was much more costly than it needed to be. The utility operated in a highly regulated environment, and audits were increasing; another utility company had recently been fined $1 million per day for inability to produce safety records relating to a fatal explosion at one of its facilities. On a day-to-day basis, employees had to search for information, causing frustration and lowered productivity.

The IM project started out with a small but visible pilot to help one of the business units manage its engineering, operating, and maintenance procedures more effectively. The same underlying technology platform used in this unit was also being used in two other ways in the enterprise—as a project management tool and as the foundation for the company's new intranet. Using her skills as a Champion—she could see the big picture and convince people to move in a new direction—Chloe, the project manager, lobbied to have both of these initiatives brought under her umbrella. She made a compelling business case and was successful. The three initiatives were officially placed under IM, which became a "program." Chloe was christened "program manager."

Chloe learned that she should've been careful what she wished for. After a few weeks, things had become challenging for her on several fronts. While she'd been engaged in strategic planning and time-consuming networking activities, other parts of the project began to fall through the cracks. Chloe liked to joke that she wasn't a very good project manager, meaning that attention to detail was not her forte. The business unit pilot was set to go live in a week, and, unfortunately, when she called a meeting with the project leads, she realized that key tasks—such as migrating information from the old system, communicating with key stakeholders, and redirecting links to the new site—hadn't been taken care of. Chloe recognized that she had spread herself too thin and neglected the basics.

Brooke was the design lead for the pilot. She had just turned twenty-nine, and this was not only her largest and most visible project but also her first time to serve as design lead and have a staff reporting to her. A Champion like Chloe, she focused much more on the aspects of the job that were enjoyable and came naturally to her—facilitating the design process and interfacing with the business leaders (that is, moving the goals of the project forward through partnering with the people)—than on the details of making sure all the *i*'s were dotted and *t*'s crossed for the testing and turnover (that is, executing the plan).

Despite the setback, launch was successful and no one outside the project team realized how narrowly they'd averted disaster. Chloe was smart and sensitive enough to realize that this was a learning and a team-building opportunity, so she convened a meeting to review the project launch. She apologized for not being more active in the project and for not supporting the team during crunch time. She offered positive and constructive feedback to each member and asked that they do the same for her and each other. The experience was helpful for all involved and resulted in new agreements for how they would handle future deployments.

One of the major factors that had distracted Chloe from the pilot launch was her focus on engaging executives in the change program. Even though the initial limited-scope project had expanded into an enterprise-wide program based on Chloe's request, and even though the CIO was a program sponsor, the executive team as a whole had never been formally briefed on the program. Therefore, several mission-critical projects that fell within the program were basically unfunded mandates. Chloe became increasingly frustrated by her inability to influence up and turned to her boss, Kevin, a vice president in IT and the CIO's second-in-command.

Kevin shared Chloe's enthusiasm for the new vision of IM at the utility. However, he had been there long enough to realize that to sell new ideas, he had to temper his style and slow his pace. While his colleagues saw Kevin as an optimist, Chloe tended to come off to their more staid peers as salesy, slick, and even a little manipulative. This was shocking to Chloe, who in all things endeavored to do the right thing, and who viewed herself as an experienced woman of substance.

By the end of year two of the IM program, the team had launched four major projects. The new portal—the most visible and first truly enterprise-wide project—was next. Although Chloe remained disappointed that she hadn't yet successfully engaged the entire executive team, she accepted that the culture was slow to change. She decided to actively work on developing her skills as an influencer, so her audience would perceive her as a passionate yet prudent leader who gets things done. She was actively receiving coaching from her boss, Kevin, and was mentoring Brooke as well.

CHLOE: THE CHAMPION PROJECT MANAGER

Chloe had successfully implemented a cloud-based solution for the utility's business contingency plans, which greatly increased the probability that the company would have the information required to weather a major catastrophe. Chloe's solution enabled the business to function through a disaster with limited interruptions of service to customers and no major hiccups in operations or other mission-critical functions. Two others had unsuccessfully attempted this IT project before Chloe, so she was already respected for her ability to get things done.

Chloe's smarts enabled her to see how the IM project was a logical extension of that first initiative, given its focus on deploying innovative new technology to enable data integrity, management, and compliance. She used her charismatic personality to capitalize upon her initial success and build relationships beyond IT and the risk management department to promote an enterprise-wide approach to technology-facilitated information management.

After combining three projects into one larger program, Chloe's next mission became tackling the fact that IT didn't have an adequate budget for the workload, and that each of the four business units were planning on following their own strategies instead of the corporate-wide approach. Chloe worked passionately to raise awareness at the executive level in order to obtain a mandate for a consistent approach and to secure adequate funding for all the critical initiatives.

However, after a point she felt stymied, frustrated by what seemed like constant roadblocks and inaction. While she made her case eloquently, emphatically, and through multiple channels, she was only getting so far, and she was starting to feel uncharacteristically burned out.

When she finally sat down with Kevin, he said that her energy was actually off-putting to some at the utility. He told her with as much tact as possible that she was moving way too fast—the utility's culture was slow moving and risk averse. Even though Chloe had been careful to frame her messages in a way that meshed with this culture—she argued that adopting the program would enhance compliance and reduce risk—the way she conveyed the messages and her overall pace and intensity were preventing people from truly appreciating the soundness of her plans.

KEVIN: THE CHAMPION EXECUTIVE

Kevin was an "enlightened" Champion who had learned the lessons Chloe was just dealing with earlier in his career. He'd been able to adapt his style to fit the more reserved culture of the utility, and he'd successfully risen to the VP level. While Chloe was laboring on IM, Kevin was spearheading a major change initiative within the IT department, implementing a project management office (PMO) and project management methodology (PMM), two firsts in its history. Disciplined project management was a strategic goal of the CEO, and Kevin linked his initiative in IT to the overall corporate objective. He helped his IT colleagues see how, although it would cost more initially in terms of start-up budget and overhead for additional staff, a more consistent and supportive approach to managing projects would ultimately enable IT to better meet its commitments to its internal customers and escalate issues that inhibited the project's progress up the chain of command for speedier resolution. Kevin and his team implemented the new PMO within nine months, and by twelve months could demonstrate its financial payback.

Kevin's success in spearheading the PMO implementation revealed his growth in another area as well. When he was a new IT project manager like Brooke, Kevin had regarded any problem that came up as a negative reflection on his leadership abilities. When trouble arose on his projects, he would try to find a solution as swiftly and quietly as possible. He would hesitate to ever escalate a problem and ask for assistance, even when it turned into an issue that was obviously impacting a project's execution.

This mindset worked for Kevin on smaller projects, but it had almost derailed his career when a major, highly visible implementation veered off path. His superior had confronted him with the many outstanding issues on the project and asked why he'd failed to escalate them, especially when there were people in the organization who could have stepped in and kept the project on track. Kevin's reluctance to do so had the same root cause as Brooke's failure to ask for help during the near miss of the project launch.

BROOKE: THE CHAMPION NEW SUPERVISOR

As a first-time design lead, Brooke had also been caught up in the excitement of the burgeoning program and her expanding role in it. She loved both the wide reach of the project—her sites would have an important bottom-line impact and make people's lives easier on the job—and the fact that she could now coach junior designers.

And she had many opportunities to coach the junior designers. The technology was new to the organization, and gathering proper requirements from end users proved challenging. It took multiple iterations to arrive at a workable solution for the pilot participants. While it wasn't unusual for designers to go through several iterations, in this case, each iteration was more like going back to the drawing board and beginning again as the end users became more aware of the full range of capabilities.

During all this back and forth, Brooke did a marvelous job keeping her team motivated. Two of the junior designers were particularly frustrated, but she helped them see that communicating with novice business users and crafting a truly customized, business-beneficial solution was a great learning experience for them.

However, all the iterations caused Brooke and her team to slip on their deliverables. Brooke had never been given any project management training to accompany her new responsibilities, and she wasn't used to being accountable for others' deadlines across multiple work streams. She got caught up in the excitement of the projects and her dealings with their many new stakeholders. Brooke felt horrible about how the pilot launch had almost been derailed by her lack of follow-through and attention to detail, after so many months of hard work by so many people.

The Champion's Strengths

Chloe displayed a classic Champion outlook when she saw the strategic benefit of merging three disparate projects under one program and then influenced others to accept this new approach. She formulated a sound business case and then boldly promoted it up, down, and across the organization. She used her verbal skills and enlightened them with her sound business rationale—a classic combination of the Heart and Head approaches.

Moreover, since Champions have both people and purpose on their radar screens, they notice when people are resisting change, and they intuitively understand why. With a firm grasp of both interpersonal dynamics and business realities, Champions can be very savvy in navigating company politics. Therefore, they are uniquely suited to craft messages that speak to various stakeholder groups in a way that addresses their needs and concerns while also maintaining a strong business focus.

As all three leaders in this case study demonstrate, Champions love to mentor people and tend to be very good at it. They genuinely care about others and their development, and they derive great satisfaction from seeing those they mentor rise. As participative team leaders, they work hard to keep people motivated during challenging times with their optimism and enthusiasm.

The Champion's Blind Spots

However, any strength overdone can become a weakness, and the Champion is no exception. While Chloe's style worked well to merge the projects, she was less successful in engaging executives and leaders of the utility's business units and convincing them to fund the program.

Meanwhile, in the implementation he handled, Kevin showed that he had overcome a detrimental aspect of his change leader style: Champions' penchant for focusing on the positive can have the effect of downplaying the severity of the negative, failing to adequately deal with the negative, or preventing team members from raising legitimate concerns.

In her learning curve as a Champion change leader, Brooke also learned that too much of a good thing can become problematic. Champions can become enamored with the next new initiative and thus neglect to follow up and finish strong on their current commitments. In her zeal to take on more responsibility, Brooke did not set appropriate priorities for herself and her staff, causing a last-minute crisis that nearly ended in disaster.

Which is exactly what Chloe did in dropping the ball on overseeing Brooke's project as the program manager. While they love to mentor,

Champions don't get as fired up about day-to-day supervisory tasks. Chloe recognized and acknowledged that fact to her staff during the project review. To her credit, she set the environment for open, safe sharing by showing her own willingness to receive feedback. Her project team then rose to the occasion.

THE CHAMPION AS A LEADER

Most of the time you . . .

- Take a lead role in change by combining your intuitive grasp of possibilities with your dynamic interpersonal style
- Are adept at verbally communicating the vision, explaining how the change will affect individuals, teams, and the organization
- Exude enthusiasm and optimism, even in the face of challenges and setbacks
- Are confident in your ability to overcome resistance and motivate people toward a goal
- Are socially skilled and relate easily to a wide variety of people

But sometimes you . . .

- Can undervalue the tactical activities necessary to accomplish a goal
- Can fail to address the requirements of others who have a greater need to know details and specifics
- Can downplay the importance of problems and risks in pursuit of a goal, being overly optimistic about the capacity of yourself and others
- Can come across as calculating, more interested in achieving your own goals rather than those of the organization or other individuals
- Can become overcommitted in too many new initiatives at once, and can get derailed from finishing one objective before becoming enamored with the next new thing

THE CHAMPION AS VIEWED BY OTHERS

Usually people see you as . . .

- Compelling
- Charismatic
- Optimistic
- Persuasive
- Enlightening

However, occasionally you are . . .

- Frustrated by others who don't think as positively as you do
- Apt to push too hard
- Overly competitive
- Manipulative
- Glib

The Champion on the Job

Let's now take a deeper dive and look at how Champions at all levels—executive, project management, and supervisory—can capitalize on their strengths and work on their weak spots.

THE CHAMPION AS A PROJECT MANAGER

Chloe was a project manager who joked that she was not a very good project manager. If you're a non-Hand-oriented PM (Champions, Coaches, and Visionaries), you may criticize yourself similarly, because many of the defining aspects of project management (planning, organizing, and accountability to timeframes, deliverables, and budgets) do not come as naturally to you as they do to other styles with a more tactical/executional bent. Nevertheless, as a Champion, you can make an exceptional PM as you help your team balance tactical tasks and deliverables with strategic goals and the people affected by them.

Strengths of the Champion Project Manager

- With your verbal skills and ability to relate to a wide range of people, you are uniquely positioned to communicate about change in a way that reaches a variety of different audiences. You utilize these skills to advocate for change across the full gamut of stakeholders impacted by the change.
- Obtaining resources is often a challenge for PMs, particularly when they're vying for the time and attention of project team members who may report to them only on a part-time basis. But you use your influence skills to negotiate priorities and expectations with your team members and their other supervisors.
- You use your ability to identify and overcome resistance to facilitate conversations within your project team, as well as between your team and the stakeholders you are impacting outside the team.

Traps Champion Project Managers Should Avoid

- Because now you may be in a position to lead and influence people of various disciplines in which you may not have deep experience, your enthusiastic style may be misinterpreted as lacking substance. Are you balancing enthusiasm with gravitas to be perceived as a grounded leader?
- As the scope of your projects and reach expands, and as you are confronted with numerous promising possibilities, you may be lured away from actions, issues, and risks. Do you capture risks and issues

in a structured manner? Do you consistently assign a responsible party to resolve them, and do you then monitor progress appropriately? Do you take time to raise difficult issues and explore them in depth? Are you sometimes tempted to downplay the seriousness of problems?

THE CHAMPION AS A NEW SUPERVISOR

When promoted to her first design lead position, Brooke was thrilled about the possibility of widening her ability to impact and influence others, but she didn't focus as much on supervising the details of the change. As a new supervisor and a Champion, when you enthusiastically take on the diverse aspects of your new role, you may have a similar realization: your staff may not be accomplishing their objectives in a timely and thorough manner because they aren't receiving detailed supervision.

Strengths of the Champion New Supervisor

- You motivate people with your passion and your focus on purpose. Just as Brooke helped her team see how they were making people's lives easier at work and helping the company remain in compliance, you inspire your staff by communicating the meaning behind even the mundane tasks in support of the change.
- With your natural confidence and charm, you identify opportunities to make presentations and be the face of change more broadly.
- Especially during the challenging times of change, your optimism is an asset. You help others find the positive in stressful times, and you are skilled at confronting and deflating rumors, pessimism, and other normal yet dysfunctional reactions.

Traps Champion New Supervisors Should Avoid

- You may be surprised that others do not share your enthusiasm and need to focus more on detailed plans, procedures, and accountabilities to ensure change happens.

- As a frontline leader, the concerns of your people are often grounded in day-to-day reality. Are you tempering your enthusiasm with a dose of realism? Do you give sufficient consideration to immediate concerns, or do you come off as glib?

- Possibilities need plans to bring them to life. In your zeal to "get there," have you remembered to lay out the *how*? Schedule some alone time to list all the tactical tasks that need to happen to ensure smooth outcomes—make sure you get them all. Then, sense-check your list with a more meticulous peer or staff member.

- Have you asked for two-way feedback from your direct reports to be sure people really understand? Champions tend to be more focused on talking than on listening. Have you actively listened to (not talked at) people to ensure they are fully on board, and not just momentarily caught up in your enthusiasm?

THE CHAMPION AS AN EXECUTIVE

Kevin, an enlightened Champion, brought decades of experience to the role and actively mentored Chloe so she could learn from his mistakes and successfully navigate the utility's political landscape. Kevin had learned to manage his presence, invite critical comments, and moderate his enthusiasm for the next exciting thing on the horizon.

Strengths of the Champion Executive

- You naturally step up to lead change by combining your intuitive grasp of possibilities with your dynamic interpersonal style.

- As the most naturally charismatic and passionate of all the styles, you are uniquely suited to help design and deliver messages about change projects. Your arguments make business sense and speak to individual people. You have the capacity to craft and communicate meaningful, moving change messages.

- There may be pockets of resistance in your organization, and your fellow executives may not be on board and aligned, but since you tend to grasp both where the change is leading and where the people are coming from, you help enlighten people about the benefits and persuade them to work through the challenges together.

Traps Champion Executives Should Avoid

- When considering a new business direction, ask yourself, "Does it make wise business sense? Is it more than just a fad?" Make sure you surround yourself with people who gravitate more toward facts and figures. Work with them to understand short-term and long-term risks and benefits.

- Are you inviting critical comments and dissenting opinions during change? And do you make time to listen to, explore, and process them?

- Have you taken the time to make genuine connections with your colleagues? Do they understand what drives you? Have you communicated your sincere intent to collaborate with them, not compete with them? Have you solicited information about what is important to them, so you can help them achieve their objectives as well? Champions can make great mentors, too. Are you actively coaching and positioning your direct reports for their future success in their careers?

The Champion: The Bottom Line

Much of the change management literature highlights the importance of change champions. Here we're focusing more on a behavioral style than on the act of championing, but there's no doubt that we need people who promote change and rally others around the initiative.

As Rosabeth Moss Kanter points out in her book *Evolve!*, "'If you can dream it, you can do it' is not necessarily true. 'If you can dream it AND make others dream it, you can do it.'"[17] Champions know this instinctively; more than any other style of change leader, they have the capacity to provide compelling, persuasive cases for their lofty dreams.

But leadership author Jim Clemmer describes some of the problems we saw when Champions didn't account for their blind spots: "Change Champions are vital learning leaders for an organization. We need their energy, ideas, and creativity today more than ever. But we have to learn how to coordinate their unbounded and disruptive zeal . . . For example . . . to understand the need for a delicate balance between change and stability."[18]

Even though Champions aren't strongest with Hands skills, they can use their gifts to encourage practical action in others. In James Kouzes and Larry Posner's *The Leadership Challenge*, one of the authors' five leadership principles is "Enable Others to Act." Champions do this naturally by fostering collaboration, creating a climate of trust, facilitating relationships, strengthening others, enhancing self-determination, and developing competence and confidence. We saw this in action with Brooke leading her new team, Chloe coaching Brooke, and Kevin mentoring Chloe.

Champions excel at leading changes that are good for people and vital for the business. They get the big picture and enthusiastically jump at new challenges. Optimistic even in the face of setbacks, they exhibit unrelenting energy as they persuade others toward positive goals.

Self-assessment Questions

If you are a very low Hands change leader, ask yourself . . .

- Do your change projects veer off course, take longer than expected, or go over budget?
- Are you ever surprised that people are not fully on board with a change process? Do you find that others act confused and don't know what to do? Could this be because you've done too much talking and not enough listening to their needs and concerns? Have you failed to show them specifically how they can help support the change process?
- Do you at times find it difficult to relate to, effectively persuade, and partner with more detailed and technically oriented people?
- Are you sometimes characterized as more of a "cheerleader" than a "champion," perhaps seen as lacking substance or as not giving sufficiently serious consideration to the difficult realities of a situation?
- Do people sometimes interpret your attempts to motivate as manipulation?

 Visit www.ChangeCatalysts.com/BookResources for additional coaching hints on how Champions can leverage their strengths and shore up their blind spots.

CHAPTER 8

THE DRIVER

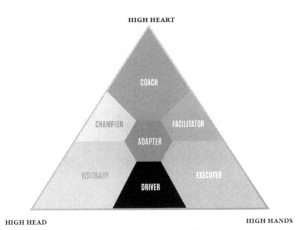

Figure 7.1: The CQ Triangle—The Driver

The Driver's Motto: Just do it! Get 'er done!

Drivers are all about results—they hunger to achieve the objectives of the change initiative. They are focused on both the short-term and long-term aspects of the change, and they will do whatever it takes to complete the immediate task and move toward the ultimate goal. They pitch in, share their expertise, and work long and hard toward objectives. But while they focus on the strategic and tactical business issues, Drivers may not give sufficient attention to the people aspects of the change process. They may be so focused on the work that they fail to raise important questions about the impact of the change on organizational culture, team dynamics, or individual people.

Get to Know Yourself as a Driver

More than any other style, the Driver wants results. You value and place a high degree of time and attention on getting the job done, simultaneously focusing on the strategic change goal as well as on the tactical plans necessary to accomplish objectives along the way. You excel at being forceful, pragmatic, and analytical.

It will come as no surprise to most Drivers that they don't always pay sufficient attention to the people side of change. You will significantly increase your ability to lead lasting, meaningful, truly impactful change by engaging more with a wide variety of stakeholders, crafting messages that connect with affected groups, and attempting to understand and alleviate people's concerns during the change process. Incorporating more genuine warmth and interest in others will help you emerge not just as a strong leader but as a caring mentor as well.

Drivers in Action

The refinery involved in this case study was facing a serious brain drain: all current maintenance personnel were set to retire within five years, and it had gone through years of downsizing with very few new hires. Todd, a young, high-potential process engineer, was appointed to lead a project team charged to figure out a solution to this problem. It was a stretch assignment intended to expand Todd's leadership talent. On the team with him were ten other participants, from company management and the union, and one of these was a supervisor named Derrick. After years as a mechanic, Derrick had recently been promoted to foreman, and he was on the team to represent his unit and the foreman group.

Derrick had been instrumental in raising the issue of the aging workforce and had succeeded in getting a team chartered to find a solution. Derrick's business sense enabled him to grasp the situation and its implications and to translate its potentially dire impact to both his bosses and union officials.

Once the project began, Todd's tactical skills kicked in. He was a major factor in the team's ability to rise to the occasion and devise two dozen potential business solutions, all consisting of staffing the maintenance function with various combinations of apprentices, journeyman, or contractors. The team made a compelling business case and presented several well-grounded solutions to the refinery's leadership team, made up of company and union representatives.

On the leadership team was Nate, the refinery's union vice president and a card-carrying pipefitter. He was part of a union leadership team that had held its position for over a decade and negotiated with management during years of tough economic times. The union leadership was known as traditional but balanced, with Nate often playing the role of bad cop to the union president's good cop.

Nate was adamantly opposed to any solution to the attrition problem that involved increasing the number of contractors and decreasing the number of in-house, proprietary journeymen—i.e., union members. However, Nate also understood the company's economic situation and the realities of the local job market. In the end, the union and company management reached a compromise: apprenticeship programs would be created for five of the most critical craft lines, with the solution for the other three lines to be decided during the next round of negotiations. Even though the decision to hire green recruits and start up five distinct apprenticeship training programs was a very expensive proposition for management, Nate explained that his union members would take an active role in training their junior peers, which helped keep on-the-job training costs lower and the project more palatable to management.

When the recommendation was accepted and the design team became an implementation team, the leadership styles of our three Drivers were stretched. While Derrick's fellow foremen acknowledged that the current workforce would retire "someday," they had a heck of a lot to do today and didn't make supervising apprentices in the field a priority. And while machinists, mechanics, electricians, instrument techs, and analyzers knew that most real craft training takes place in the field not in the classroom, what was in it for them to train others? They weren't getting paid for it. And many simply didn't know how to train.

In retrospect, the team realized that many of these concerns had been raised during the design process, but they hadn't given them sufficient attention. Todd saw these "people issues" as tangential, and consistently refocused the team on metrics and tactics.

Ultimately, the apprentice program was implemented successfully, so much so that it was re-implemented at another one of the global energy firm's U.S. refineries. The joint union-management team even made presentations about the program at industry conferences. However, the project had taken a lot longer than it needed to due to additional, unplanned activities. The team had had to devise new systems to plan apprentice rotations, balance maintenance workload with on-the-job training, and establish a mentoring program to teach journeymen how to train their junior peers. All of this was the result of taking insufficient account of people's fears, team norms, and cultural dynamics. At the outset of the project, the team's Drivers hadn't seen the fundamental importance of these issues.

DERRICK: THE DRIVER NEW SUPERVISOR

Derrick exuded dynamic passion for the job. He understood how the maintenance work done by his team fit into making the refinery a high-reliability organization, and he knew the numbers like the back of his hand. A former marine who definitely looked the part, Derrick was barrel-chested with a booming voice—an imposing boss to say the least. While other foremen frequently complained about the "entitlement mentality" of new recruits and the slack work habits of more senior employees getting ready to retire, all of Derrick's people worked hard for him. He set high standards, provided clear expectations, and relentlessly held people accountable.

When the time came to "work the plan," Derrick had faith in their approach and was extremely motivated to present it to his peers and the troops so they could get to work. Much to his surprise and dismay, the others weren't nearly as enthusiastic as he.

When it came to implementing peer-to-peer on-the-job training between apprentices and senior journeymen, Derrick found his "just do it" style lacking. He was used to giving task assignments, monitoring performance, and ensuring completion. However, when he began hearing from some apprentices that their mentors treated them like gophers, using them to fetch tools and climb ladders with no training interaction, Derrick was at a loss for how to coach his former peers. He was frustrated by the idea of having to babysit them; he didn't have the time to make sure they were transferring knowledge, not hoarding it.

Likewise, he found it was a challenge to deal with his fellow foremen and planners. The schedules they created and managed made maintenance work the sole priority, constantly overriding training time in favor of the crisis of the day. And since Derrick had no formal authority over them, it proved difficult for him to change this dynamic.

Finally, when he reached his wit's end, Derrick realized that issuing orders was not a winning tactic. Instead, he began to flex a new set of muscles—he started asking questions and listening to the answers. That's how he really began to understand the world from others' perspectives, which enabled him to bring valuable insights to the implementation team.

TODD: THE DRIVER PROJECT MANAGER

Todd, the process engineer on the unit Derrick's team supports, was a Desert Storm veteran who shared many aspects of Derrick's style, chief among them a penchant for efficient planning and acting with a sense of urgency. The two respected each other (even though one's army and the other's marines) and made a forceful pair leading the refinery's Alkylation ("Alky") unit. Even though Todd was relatively young, he played a project management role in several successful turnarounds (multimillion-dollar shutdowns to perform maintenance and technical upgrades) and was as comfortable presenting to the refinery's leadership team as he was running his work area's morning meeting and reviewing the previous day's safety and efficiency results.

Todd ran the project team meetings like he did turnaround meetings, with structure and intention. He kept the group focused and sidebars to a minimum. He tended to cut off topics he perceived as tangential and steer the team back to the agenda.

Often, though, those "tangential" topics had to do with people stuff. As a Driver PM, Todd needed to learn that the human side was not tangential, soft, or irrelevant. In fact, people's resistance to the change initiative proved to be the major challenge, eclipsing budget and resources. Todd found that facilitating a project team is very different than managing a turnaround, where the goals and process are typically much more objective and mutually understood. While unpredictable problems arose during a turnaround, they were largely of a technical nature, and when people issues came up, they usually concerned personnel availability. Had Todd allowed the deeper people stuff to surface in meetings of the project team during the design stage, and had he probed and dealt with them, the implementation stage would have been much smoother.

NATE: THE DRIVER EXECUTIVE

One of the problems that surfaced during implementation was the fact that the majority of journeymen felt uncomfortable as trainers, and the majority of foremen didn't know how to support them in this new role. The implementation team soon realized they needed to provide "train the trainer" classes for the journeymen. The team brought in an outside training firm, who recommended starting the sessions by focusing on the journeymen's main question: "What's in it for me to train apprentices?" The facilitators suggested an exercise in which the journeymen would share stories about how they were mentored early in their careers, to tease out the lesson that such relationships were vital. The facilitators wanted everyone to see that mentoring isn't only about transferring technical skills, but also about building trusting relationships.

When the facilitators presented the leadership team with a dry run of this exercise, Nate balked. He said his people would never participate in such a touchy-feely exercise. So he was blown away when instead of the fifteen minutes devoted to this exercise during the first official session, it took an hour and a half. Each journeyman spoke for an average of five minutes and told their very heartfelt story. One electrician who'd been at the refinery for thirty years talked about how his mentor had given him a book his first day on the job and said, "Here is everything you need to know about electricity." This mentor then proceeded to spend the next three years walking the electrician through the book while they partnered on their tasks. One black woman shared an "anti-mentor" story about how difficult it had been when she started as the first woman and one of only three minority crafts persons at the refinery and had no one there to support her. The experience was an epiphany not just for Nate but for everyone who attended as well. Human beings bring their brains and brawns to the workplace as well as their hearts and hopes.

The Driver's Strengths

Drivers make things happen. Derrick, Todd, and Nate saw a problem and put together a plan to fix it. "Brain drain"—the exodus of senior, highly trained employees—in industrial workplaces is a nationwide problem, and few firms take proactive steps to address it. These three, however, demonstrated an ability to step outside their day-to-day roles, look into the future, and come up with strategies for how to make their workplace a better one. And they each had an excellent grasp of the day-to-day realities of their company and saw the specific, tactical steps that would take them from here to there.

Each took positive steps to "get 'er done" at their level. Derrick, on the front lines, saw the impact of the aging workforce firsthand, from the increasing number of retiring journeymen to the multitudinous age-related injuries and lowered productivity (old-timers weren't as quick to climb multistory ladders and take on other physically demanding tasks). Even before he transitioned to management, Derrick initiated conversations about attrition and its impact during union meetings, and was pivotal in getting the initiative launched.

Todd capitalized on the skills he had picked up while managing turn-arounds to lead his team toward detailed solutions that not only solved the problem but also delineated pros and cons and implementation tactics. He kept the team on track and focused, even when there were heated differences of opinion between union representatives and company management. His blunt, no-nonsense style worked well in these situations.

As a union leader, Nate never lost sight of his primary objective—to maintain the strength of the union membership, which had been in decline since the 1980s. However, he was able to balance the union's goal with the realities faced by management and negotiate a plan that furthered both sets of interests, promoted the long-term health of the refinery, and made good business sense.

The Driver's Blind Spots

While the project team's vision was right on target, they forgot a crucial step: bringing other people along! The plan was logical, but it didn't account for the needs and fears of the people who were key to bringing it to life. Instead, the leaders' unstated philosophy was that everyone would have to "learn it, live it, love it"—a favorite expression from Todd's and Derrick's military background. When Derrick brought the challenges he was facing to one of the implementation team meetings, Todd remembered that some of his fellow team members had voiced concerns during the design phase about how the new program would be received by workers on the front lines. However, these team members were too intimidated to push the issue, fearing their perspective would be discounted and that they'd be seen as soft.

Similarly, Nate didn't consider the emotional reactions his union members would have when told they were expected to train junior peers. He looked at this as purely a compensation issue that would be addressed in the next set of negotiations, where the plan was to bargain for additional remuneration for several new responsibilities that the company was asking journeymen to take on. But while they may have wanted to be mentors and participate in training the new generation, many journeymen feared looking stupid in front of younger, more computer-savvy new recruits. These fears and insecurities about the situation didn't occur to Nate.

By not understanding the goals and emotions of others, these three Drivers unintentionally missed a wide array of critical factors as they designed their solution to the attrition problem and planned its implementation.

THE DRIVER AS A LEADER

Most of the time you . . .

- Have a keen grasp of strategy and execution
- Know where you want to go and how you need to get there, and are able to focus on both the what and the how of change
- Are tireless in pursuit of goals
- Balance dealing with current state while putting systems and processes in place to move the organization toward the future
- Are not afraid to face brutal facts and confront harsh realities

But sometimes you . . .

- May not give sufficient attention to the cultural components of change
- May not appear to focus adequately on people's individual needs or on team dynamics
- Complain about lack of progress toward goals and the less-than-optimal efforts of others
- Do not give sufficient attention to the process by which goals are reached
- Can seem less interested in obtaining buy-in from others, incorporating their opinions into solutions and strategies, or engaging in two-way dialogue with them

THE DRIVER AS VIEWED BY OTHERS

Usually people see you as . . .
• Confident
• Intentional
• Focused
• Pragmatic
• Analytical
However, occasionally you are . . .
• Overly direct
• A poor listener
• Stubborn
• Controlling
• Unrelenting

The Driver on the Job

Let's now take a deeper dive and look at how Drivers at all levels—executive, project management, and supervisory—can capitalize on their strengths and work on their weak spots.

THE DRIVER AS A NEW SUPERVISOR

As a Driver and a strong technical performer with a solid work ethic, Derrick brought his "marine mentality" to the table. He could get people moving and get things done. Similarly, you may view stepping up to supervisor as a way to get important goals achieved in your work area. Also like Derrick, when presented with the challenge of supervising employees' day-to-day work while leading difficult changes, you may need to work on your listening and engagement skills.

Strengths of the Driver New Supervisor

- Often, you were the go-to individual contributor who has now risen to the go-to supervisor. You'll be able to leverage your focused and forceful nature to achieve the goals of the change process.
- You are the most conflict tolerant of all styles of change leader. Since you're not afraid to take on a tough challenge, you can confront others who are standing in the way of positive change, hold a mirror to their face so they see their negative impact, and reverse their dysfunctional behavior.
- Many Drivers step up into management because they are frustrated with the inefficiencies they see in their work area. Now that you have the formal position, you can use your analytical skills and your zeal for challenging the status quo to eradicate barriers to moving forward.

Traps Driver New Supervisors Should Avoid

- You may be frustrated by the need to babysit others and to listen to their needs and concerns. But remember, leading people is not babysitting. How can you make it a priority to develop active listening skills, ask questions, and allow for constructive interaction?
- People perform better when they know why they're being asked to do something. Have you taken the time to explain the rationale behind asking people to change, rather than just issuing orders?
- It's not just what you say, but how you say it. How can you moderate your tone and body language to be more open to less aggressive styles? Try telling a joke. Flash that winning smile.

- Do you know your coworkers as individuals? Change can bring up
  fears and insecurities in many people. You are leading people with
  their own dreams and motivations, not just doers of tasks. Make
  time to informally walk around without an agenda.

THE DRIVER AS A PROJECT MANAGER

Todd was an exceptional turnaround manager who realized that to lead
other types of project teams, he needed to do more than just get things
done—he had to get them done right. As a Driver project manager, you
may also benefit from learning this lesson. To achieve the change objective, you need to bring your project team members and the full array of
impacted stakeholders along with you on your mission.

Strengths of the Driver Project Manager

- The most pragmatic of any style of change leader, you focus your
  team on the most efficient tactics to get your project from here to
  there, making you a very effective PM.
- Your relentless attention to results is a significant plus on change
  projects, especially those involving challenging demands and tight
  deadlines.
- Since you do not shy away from conflict or from accepting responsibility, you are more comfortable than most in saying what needs to
  be said when change processes are veering off course. You help others
  involved in the change process get back on track.

Traps Driver Project Managers Should Avoid

- Does your direct and straightforward communication style come
  across as blunt or intimidating to others? Do you sometimes prevent

airing of opinions and alternatives because of how you come across? How can you remind yourself to ask more questions, and really listen before you respond?

- Since you love to win, you love to keep score. This is an area that can challenge other styles. How can you devise systems to keep score *and* share the score?

- Are your people exhausted, stressed, or overwhelmed? Are the pace of change and your high expectations negatively affecting quality or quantity of output? Are your team members able to juggle their role on the project team with the other responsibilities on their plates?

- As the saying goes, sometimes we need to go slow to go fast, to power down to power up. Make sure you keep team dynamics on your radar screen. Do you need to take a time-out to check in with people, to see how they are doing, make sure their needs and concerns are being addressed, and confirm they feel like valued and contributing members of the team?

THE DRIVER AS AN EXECUTIVE

Drivers relish positions of power and authority. Nate co-led the union through some of the most challenging times in its history, balancing a focus on the union's objectives (maintaining membership and fair treatment of its workers) with management's objectives (maintaining a profitable operation and a competitive position in the market). As an executive Driver, you need to keep the organization moving forward while at the same time maintaining a healthy organizational climate, where people are committed to their work and feel like they're growing with the company.

Strengths of the Driver Executive

- You have a unique ability to simultaneously lead strategic deliberations while keeping a firm grasp on tactical details. You remain future-focused yet pragmatic. You're in touch without micromanaging.

- As a Driver, you are probably the prototypical hard-driving executive. Your no-nonsense style helps your executive team remain focused on the most efficient and practical solutions to change challenges.

- Drivers have a palpable sense of urgency. You work to ensure that your organization perceives the need for change as urgently as you do and that the necessary parties are motivated to take decisive action.

- When a change process is most challenging, you are often out in front, if not at the helm, navigating to get back on course. It's you who steps up to take charge of change.

Traps Driver Executives Should Avoid

- Drivers at the top are particularly prone to being isolated from the impact of change at lower levels in their organizations. Due to their intimidating style, others are often hesitant to tell Drivers what is really going on. Is your leadership style preventing people from giving you information you need to hear?

- Executives are in a unique position to allocate resources and mandate alterations to systems that interfere with change. How can you ensure that organizational systems are supportive of change? If they're not aligned, the change project is likely to fail.

- Looking back on their working lives, many people point to mentoring others as the most fulfilling aspects of their careers. Most Drivers tend to overlook these opportunities. Are there people in your organization or industry who could benefit from your wisdom and experience?
- Similarly, are you making your organization a place where people feel fulfilled, a place where people want to work? Make it a priority to periodically assess the state of your organization's culture, particularly the level of engagement of your employees and their connection with the company's mission and values.

The Driver: The Bottom Line

In the classic business book *In Search of Excellence,* Tom Peters and Robert H. Waterman Jr. list eight principles of excellent, innovative companies. The first is "A bias for action, for getting on with it." Drivers have that nailed!

But a key challenge for Drivers is to, as John Kotter puts it in his book *The Heart of Change,* "increase the sense of urgency" in others. Kotter writes that leaders need to "raise a feeling of urgency so that people start telling each other 'we must do something' about the problems and opportunities." Kotter recommends "reducing the complacency, fear, and anger that prevent change from starting."[19] To do so, Drivers must consider the emotions of others. Particularly for technically oriented Drivers, it can be useful to remember to see emotions—both your own and others'—as data. To collect this data, Drivers benefit from "managing by walking around," soliciting information about what people are thinking and feeling. Such data often proves invaluable in leading change.

It's been said that the longest journey a person must take is the eighteen inches from his head to his heart, and that can be particularly true for Drivers. In *Beyond the Wall of Resistance*, Rick Maurer lists "failing to appreciate the power of fear" as one of the top mistakes leaders make that results in resistance to change. He goes on to say that "when fears are triggered, humans' ability to take in information goes down. In other words, people can't hear what we're talking about even if they try."[20] When Drivers don't balance their forceful style and sense of urgency with people smarts, they can scare people into ineffectiveness.

Because of their natural bias for fast, effective action, many Drivers see involving people and listening to their fears as an impediment, a slowing down. And yet, when they can overcome this reluctance, they discover that better ideas emerge and that people work hard in support of the leader and the change.

Self-assessment Questions

If you are a very low Heart change leader, ask yourself . . .

- Do others seem disconnected from the change? Do they seem unmotivated or even indifferent?
- Do you get results but sometimes realize that you've left others behind?
- Do people shy away from speaking the truth, telling you disappointing facts, or offering differing opinions because they are concerned about your reaction?
- Are your people exhausted, stressed, or overwhelmed?
- Do people respect you as a leader but fail to view you as a mentor?

Visit www.ChangeCatalysts.com/BookResources for additional coaching hints on how Drivers can leverage their strengths and shore up their blind spots.

CHAPTER 9

THE FACILITATOR

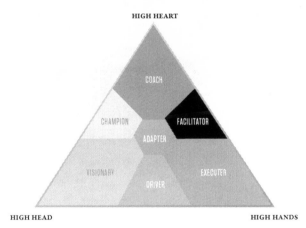

Figure 9.1: The CQ Triangle—The Facilitator

The Facilitator's Motto: I'm here to help! Lean on me.

Facilitators excel at Heart and Hands, and some say this is the best of all possible combinations, because they emphasize both task and process—they make change happen and care about how it happens. Facilitators foster change by encouraging involvement, using their listening skills, and adroitly resolving differences. At times, however, they may lose sight of the big picture and forget where the change process is ultimately leading. Facilitators may also be reluctant to provide constructive criticism for fear of disrupting relationships.

Get to Know Yourself as a Facilitator

More than any other style of change leader, you are adept at "facilitating," making the change process smooth and helping others through it. You ensure that change happens day by day, and you notice how the change process affects everyone around you. You are participative, involved, and resourceful.

As a Facilitator, you have a handle on short-term change objectives, but you may not be as good at keeping an eye on long-term business goals. A broader, more strategic view will likely make you a more effective leader, helping ensure that the actions that make up the project plan align with the ultimate destination. At times you may need to step out of your comfort zone to confront people who are not behaving consistently with the change, and you'll have to remember not to take on too many tasks yourself.

Facilitators in Action

This case study involves the start-up of a chemical-processing company. The plant's management was committed to building a participative, high-performance work culture, and the company's vision statement said, "The commitment and involvement of our team members is essential to our success. This will create an environment that promotes personal growth, secure employment, and a clean and safe workplace. Team members are the basis of our competitive advantage."

Lauren, vice president of human resources and an engineer by training, took on the task of mentoring Hanna, a young industrial engineer who gravitated to the "people side" of the start-up. Lauren was the sponsor and Hanna the project manager for an initiative to create self-directed teams during the start-up. Both women drank up their new roles. They relished overseeing the hiring process for the production and maintenance teams, onboarding new employees, and training them in both technical and team skills.

One of Lauren and Hanna's first hires was Carlos, brought in to be operations supervisor. Carlos had worked for over a decade as an hourly team leader in the start-up's parent firm, from which some of the new hires were chosen after a rigorous selection process. He relished designing exercises to stimulate the flow of creative ideas and brainstorming solutions to problems with the teams that would be implementing them.

The main construction firm involved in the start-up told the leadership team how impressed they were by the involvement of the frontline workers. They commented that they had never seen people so new to the industry offer so many innovative and sound suggestions.

Yet while Lauren was highly regarded by those below her, her peers in the leadership team never accorded her the same level of respect. Owen, vice president of operations, characterized her self-directed team project as "an asylum run by the inmates." Lauren was the staunchest promoter of a participative work culture on the leadership team, but she struggled to articulate the business rationale behind her convictions.

Immediately after the successful start-up, Owen lobbied for the company to infiltrate new markets with its products. This required that materials be made to new specifications, and the plant struggled to meet them.

Lauren advocated for elongating the timeline to give the plant time to operate in a steady state for a solid six months. She wanted to work with teams and empower them to adjust to the new operating parameters, which she was certain they could do with the right coaching.

Owen sprung on the perceived weakness of the self-directed team concept. "With strong leadership," he remarked, "everyone would be getting on the playing field and starting to make touchdowns instead of huddling in the break room sipping coffee and wasting time." Lauren couldn't convince him that the start-up wasn't truly over, that while the plant systems were running, the people systems still needed time to coalesce.

Against Lauren's wishes the decision was made to move forward with new product lines. It fell largely upon Hanna, Carlos, and the other supervisors to get frontline workers up to speed and implement the new work practices.

Carlos was actually excited by the challenge of the new product line. He got right to it, enlisting other employees to help him revise standard operating procedures, spec sheets, and the like. However, to his shock and dismay, hardly anyone seemed to be stepping up. After all the training and coaching they had given people to participate in the management-level activities, he couldn't figure out what was going on.

Hanna kept her nose to the grindstone, working with the training vendor in the classroom as well as the people in the field. She continued to do her best to provide the people the information, tools, and support they needed. Yet while Hanna was so diligently focused on the plant and frontline workers, she completely lost focus on the folks across the street in the administration building. She kept Lauren abreast of her activities but left it to the training vendor to report to the leadership team about their progress.

After a year passed, Lauren announced her departure. She accepted a new position back at the parent company to spearhead an environmental cleanup team that would work on reclaiming wetlands impacted by the company over its decades of operation. She was proud of what she achieved in the chemical plant, reconciled to the fact that she would never feel at home on the leadership team, and committed to continue her value-based work. She was ready to switch gears from promoting workplace engagement to promoting environmental stewardship.

Both Lauren and Hanna and, indeed, virtually everyone in the plant assumed Hanna would be promoted to Lauren's position. After all, Lauren had mentored her and Hanna had been accountable for nearly every aspect of the plant's human resources. Yet Hanna wasn't even given the opportunity to apply for the position. She left the firm to become the HR manager at a plastics plant in the area.

The new HR manager hired after Lauren's and Hanna's departures shared the vision of self-directed teams, but the leadership team made changes to curtail the frontline employees' scope of authority, assigning more accountability back to the supervisors. Though it fell short of the original vision, the plant is still highly participative by most standards and remains a positive place to work.

HANNA: THE FACILITATOR PROJECT MANAGER

Hanna was thrilled that her first position out of college was to help start up a new facility. Talk about a steep learning curve! She was responsible for helping install and test many of the plant's critical systems in her initial engineering role, and she was even more excited about transitioning to the people side of the start-up and the opportunity to be mentored by Lauren; Hanna aspired to a very similar career path.

Hanna partnered with the team-skills training vendor to develop and deliver most of the training the teams and supervisors received. She loved being hands-on, whether it was behind the scenes making sure training was well-designed and smoothly delivered, or whether it was supporting supervisors and employees as they applied their new skills to the job after the sessions were over. It was important to Hanna that training be fun, engaging, and applicable to frontline workers' daily life.

After a year, Hanna had practically relocated from her office in the administration building to the plant's control room. The year had been quite a success, even with the struggle of switching gears to a new product line so soon after the initial start-up.

However, Hanna had failed to build relationships with the rest of the senior team. Lauren sang her praises, but Lauren was seen by some as apt to paint a rosy picture of all plant personnel. And it was representatives of the training vendor who expanded their scope to assist with a wider range of human-resource processes and who interfaced with the senior leaders. That gave the appearance that it was the vendor team that spearheaded much of the people side of the start-up, with Hanna (and Lauren) merely playing support roles.

While responsible for so much of the plant's success, Hanna never received the recognition she deserved. Realizing that she was unlikely to be perceived as a peer by the company's senior team, she felt her only path into the managerial ranks was to transition to another firm.

LAUREN: THE FACILITATOR EXECUTIVE

Interacting with people at all levels in the plant as they put together and executed their plan was an energizing experience for Lauren. She was thrilled to have a mentee, particularly one as skilled and enthusiastic as Hanna. Lauren could be found laboring at all hours—days, nights, and weekends—as she helped teams work through people issues and technical problems, deploying both her leadership skills and her decades of engineering experience. She was appreciated by technicians, supervisors, and engineers as the most approachable and consistently positive member of the plant's leadership team.

Lauren and Owen, however, were like oil and water. Owen was an autocratic, my-way-or-the-highway thirty-year veteran of the chemical processing industry. He had been selected for his current position not for his leadership skills but because he would be the most operationally and technically experienced member of the group, a good balance to the rest of his younger, greener leadership team.

Try as she might, Lauren couldn't shift Owen's negative attitude toward self-directed teams. She could spend all day repeating statistics about the bottom-line benefits other manufacturing facilities had reaped by implementing such a culture—benefits in productivity, quality, and safety—but Owen wouldn't budge. His attitude was "I'm from Missouri. Show me—here."

In the end, Lauren's in-the-trenches, participative, and well-planned approach did not mesh well with other powerful leaders, who were more future-focused, individualistic, and entrepreneurial, and who held more sway with the CEO. While she provided a caring and concerned bridge between the administrative team and the plant team, she couldn't bridge the gaps with her executive peers.

CARLOS: THE FACILITATOR NEW SUPERVISOR

Before the project began, the start-up team made a presentation at the plant's parent company to announce the plan to build a new facility and tell current employees that they could apply for positions. Not only would the new plant have state-of-the-art equipment, the team said, it would also be run as a "high-performance, self-directed, team-based organization." The management approach would be highly participative, people at all levels would be involved in decision making, and a pay-for-performance incentive system would ensure that everyone reaped the benefits of a successful operation.

Carlos remarked that hearing the presentation was like "seeing Moses come down from the mountain." He immediately gravitated to the commandments about continuous improvement and teamwork. In his heart, he'd always known that that's how plants should operate. And now, here was a real vision of exactly how it could be carried out. He bolted up to the podium after the presentation and told Lauren he wanted to be first in line to apply. Carlos was the first supervisor they hired.

Carlos loved running team meetings. It was so refreshing, so different from what he had experienced at the parent company for the first decade of his career. For years, he had come to work, gotten handed the schedule for the day, made assignments, covered for break times, handed off to the incoming team leader, and gone home. People on his shift brought their brawn to the job but checked their brains at the door.

Yet those same workers would go home, invest in the stock market, coach their kids' soccer teams, run retreats at their churches—they were involved in a variety of creative pursuits for themselves, their families, and their communities. But at work they were treated like cogs in a machine, and they definitely lived *down* to those expectations. Joining the new team was a chance to "mine the gold in the group."

After the successful start-up, Carlos discovered that people were slipping on the fundamentals. Basic housekeeping was suffering, which could easily lead to safety hazards. The off-shifts were getting slack in completing their paperwork. And this was even before the edict came that they were to add new product lines.

Carlos tried to rally and encourage his team. And at the same time, he continued to do more and more himself. He didn't want to turn into one of those "kick butt and take names" supervisors, so while he insisted that people do the basics, he took on more and more of the supposedly self-directed team's work himself.

Perhaps the training hadn't stuck, Carlos thought. So he worked with Hanna to do another round of training and procedure writing, in which they did hands-on exercises focused on the new product line and the self-directed approach. Outside the classroom, though, much more needed to be done by his employees, and it still wasn't happening.

Carlos became increasingly resentful, frustrated that people seemed to have forgotten the vision of a participative culture. After three months, Carlos was officially burned out. He ended up with walking pneumonia and was off work for two weeks. His absence highlighted all that he had been taking on and caused Hanna and Lauren to take a serious look at how the teams were operating, how the people were feeling, and what changes they could make to steer the culture back on course.

After Lauren and Hanna departed, Carlos partnered with the new HR manager to adjust the balance of workload and accountabilities between supervisors and frontline employees. Though the new arrangement wasn't utopia, Carlos was able to take pride in the fact that the plant remained much more self-directed than most, and that by and large his people performed their expanded roles with excellence.

The Facilitator's Strengths

Facilitators share a passion for people and process. Lauren brought her love of mentoring and supporting people to her role as executive. As such, she was loved by those who reported to her. Hanna was thrilled to evolve into a "people engineer" and create organizational and training systems that would help her teams excel. Carlos provided his people with the tools they needed to get the job done.

All three demonstrate how Facilitators do not hesitate to pitch in and give as much assistance as needed. They roll up their sleeves and partner up, down, and across the organization to get things done.

Facilitators can be very creative in how they carry out their assignments. They can invent new procedures and processes to increase cooperation among employees, to manage to the plan, and to stay on track to meet their objectives.

The Facilitator's Blind Spots

In their zeal for the here and now, Facilitators can lose sight of the future. Since they can be selfless, often one of the first things they drop is any concern for their own careers. They often let proactive self-promotion fall by the wayside. Both Lauren and Hanna demonstrate the negative effects of this trait.

Taking on so much themselves can exhaust Facilitators and prevent those under them from fulfilling their own responsibilities. While noble at times, Carlos took on too much, causing his health to suffer. Moreover, his massive workload masked fundamental flaws in the self-directed system (as implemented by this plant) and prevented the organization from recognizing that changes needed to be made.

Facilitators can also struggle with communicating in business terms, particularly at the executive level. While respected for her values and skills by some of her peers, Lauren struggled to contribute on par with her fellow executives due to a perceived lack of business acumen. At the project level, Facilitators can get so caught up in the day-to-day that they overlook the political benefits of keeping key stakeholders apprised of activities, as was the case with Hanna.

THE FACILITATOR AS A LEADER

Most of the time you . . .

- Are a participative, facilitative leader
- Encourage others to work together toward goals in a structured and well-planned manner
- Are creative in partnering with others to invent new ways to accomplish objectives
- Demonstrate a can-do attitude and sincere willingness to roll up your sleeves and work alongside others to get things done
- Actively seek to provide people with the tools, training, and support they need

But sometimes you . . .

- Focus more on the immediate what and how instead of the long-term and bottom-line why
- Can get caught up in the process of making the change happen and not devote time to periodically revisiting whether the plan and path still make sense as things evolve
- Can take on too much yourself
- May not aggressively coach and deal with underperformers and those resisting the change
- May not consistently appear savvy in communicating the vision, strategy, and business case

THE FACILITATOR AS VIEWED BY OTHERS

Usually people see you as . . .

- Involved
- A good listener
- Helpful
- Resourceful
- Practical

However, occasionally you are . . .

- Too tactical
- Too focused on the here and now
- Apt to do too much yourself
- Hesitant to confront others
- Less mindful of positioning yourself as a strategic leader

The Facilitator on the Job

Let's now take a deeper dive and look at how Facilitators at all levels—executive, project management, and supervisory—can capitalize on their strengths and work on their weak spots.

THE FACILITATOR AS A NEW SUPERVISOR

When stepping up to the role of supervisor during a time of change, Facilitators can leverage many of their natural talents, but they should realize that they need to develop muscle in other areas as well.

Strengths of the Facilitator New Supervisor
- You help others by listening and providing practical, tangible advice on how to cope with change. This is your chance to be the supervisor you always wanted to have and provide people the training and tools they need.
- You show people the way by working alongside them in the early stages of a transition process, and they see that you are actively trying to remove barriers that prevent people from working consistently with the change.
- You encourage accountability by jointly devising ways for the team to self-monitor its progress.

Traps Facilitator New Supervisors Should Avoid
- Are you discouraging the hard workers on your team by allowing others to slide? How can you ensure that you're holding everyone to consistent expectations during the change process?
- You're not doing yourself any favors by taking on too much work. How can you strike an appropriate balance between lending a hand and being the leader? How can you transition from doer to delegator?
- Carlos's people lost sight of the *why*, the vision of self-direction. How can you be sure you are keeping the big-picture goals at the forefront, which can be more compelling than simply focusing on the *how*?

THE FACILITATOR AS A PROJECT MANAGER

Hanna deployed all her people and process skills to excel as a project manager. But what did she do to enhance her career? Facilitators as project managers must make time to focus on the future even as they work in the present, and they must remember to connect outside the team even as they manage inside it.

Strengths of the Facilitator Project Manager

- You help people organize themselves and coordinate their activities to meet their goal in the most efficient way.
- You help people see that the team's manager is actively soliciting and testing new ideas and approaches.
- You remind yourself to periodically meet with project sponsors to ensure that they are aware of the project's status, are supportive of your efforts, and are available to provide resources and remove barriers when necessary.

Traps Facilitator Project Managers Should Avoid

- Is your team working hard but not producing the results you want? Is it time to revisit whether you're on track to meet the right goals?
- Are you working with your team but finding that you feel isolated from everyone else? Do others know what you're up to? Have you involved outside groups and key stakeholders?
- What are you learning on the project? How are you making a difference? No doubt you have created inventive solutions to problems you've faced along the change path; how can you parlay that success into healthy self-promotion?

THE FACILITATOR AS AN EXECUTIVE

Lauren was highly respected by her employees but less consistently so by her executive peers. Executive facilitators can make participative and pragmatic leadership team members, but they may need to be mindful of opportunities to develop and demonstrate their business acumen.

Strengths of the Facilitator Executive

- You keep executive teams grounded, and you follow processes that work for the people who use them.
- You help your fellow executives work together to lead change in a way that balances raw execution with the process and effects of execution. You leverage your supportive listening skills to help your senior team resolve differences and promote active involvement.
- You help ensure that change occurs throughout the organization in a realistic, structured manner that maximizes involvement and minimizes negative impact.

Traps Facilitator Executives Should Avoid

- How can you firmly show that you've made the transition from supportive team player to strategic team leader?
- How can you make it a practice to keep up with trends that affect your industry? Can you communicate convincingly how those trends relate to changes occurring in your organization?
- How can you speak the language of strategy in addition to that of tactics, of purpose in addition to plans?
- How can you devote time for yourself and your team to periodically envision the future, imagine possibilities, and avert potential problems?

The Facilitator: The Bottom Line

High-performance, high-participation organizations display constancy of vision and flexibility of approach. That's good news for Facilitators, who excel at practical, creative, hands-on change leadership.

In *The Heart of Change*, Kotter writes,

> People change what they do less because they are given *analysis* that shifts their *thinking* than because they are *shown* a truth that influences their *feelings*. The central challenge is not strategy, not systems, not culture. These elements and many others can be very important, but the core problem without question is behavior—what people do, and the need for significant shifts in what people do . . . Changing behavior is less a matter of giving people analysis to influence their thoughts than helping to see a truth to influence their feelings. Both thinking and feeling are essential, and both are to be found in successful organizations, but the heart of change is in the emotions. The flow of see-feel-change is more powerful than that of analysis-think-change.[21]

Given their penchant for "making it real," Facilitators are naturally gifted in helping others see and feel the positive impacts of change, and as Kotter notes, this is pivotal in organizational transformation. Once a Facilitator bolsters his strong focus on the Heart and Hands with conscious attention to the Head, he'll be ready to lead positive change and invigorate his career.

Self-assessment Questions

If you are a very low Head change leader, ask yourself . . .

- Do you sometimes forget to revisit the big-picture goals of a change initiative?
- Are your people working really hard but on efforts that seem to be misplaced?
- Are you seen as more of a facilitator than a strategic leader or as more of a supportive team player than a strong manager?
- Do you sometimes feel exhausted and overwhelmed because you've taken on too much?
- Do you find that you're reluctant to confront others, even when doing so would help everyone progress toward a goal?

 Visit www.ChangeCatalysts.com/BookResources for additional coaching hints on how Facilitators can leverage their strengths and shore up their blind spots.

CHAPTER 10

THE ADAPTER

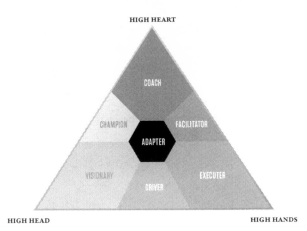

Figure 10.1: The CQ Triangle—The Adapter

The Adapter's Motto: It looks exciting. Let's all try it!

Adapters exist at the crossroads between Head, Heart, and Hands. They have a uniform score on all three dimensions. They can easily employ all three—each as it is needed—without being committed to one; and they relate well to others. But Adapters' impact as change leaders may actually be lessened because of their lack of a preference for one type. While the capacity to flex one's approach is generally an asset, at times others can find it difficult to relate to Adapters because of their changeability.

Get to Know Yourself as an Adapter

Because you are naturally skilled at utilizing all the tools in the change leader toolkit, you connect with a wide variety of stakeholders in the change process and are comfortable experimenting with creative ways to move the process forward. You excel at flexibility, inventiveness, and teamwork.

But people may find you hard to read because of your lack of a dominant change leadership style, and you may sometimes struggle with which path to pursue because of your versatility. Your genuine adaptability coupled with your desire to be part of the group can sometimes cause you to focus too much on compromise—at the expense of advocating for tough stances, at least in the short term. You're also adept at promoting change behind the scenes, but you would do well to ensure that such behavior is perceived positively by others and not as divisive scheming.

Adapters in Action

This case study involves a retail organization that operates several dozen stores in the American South and Southwest. The firm started as a mom-and-pop shop and grew by acquisition, emerging in the last decade as a well-known retailer in several regional markets.

The firm was transitioning from its entrepreneurial stage to one in which its leaders recognized the need to adopt more consistent and professional systems and processes, which is one reason Justin, the new vice president of sales, was hired. Previously, he had been a very successful sales director at a much larger competitor.

As he got to know his new team, Justin met Courtney, sales manager for the Dallas region. They hit it off immediately, sharing the same openness and easy humor. Courtney peppered Justin with questions about himself, his career path, and how he had won his current position. She half-joked that he should watch out, because she wanted to have his position one day.

Liking Courtney's ambition, Justin asked what she was doing to ready herself to move ahead in the firm. During the ensuing conversation, it became apparent that Courtney was doing the best she could where she was, but she had no idea how to become more visible to corporate leadership. The company provided sales-training events once or twice a year, but beyond that, there was no formal plan for learning and development. The firm had instituted performance evaluations the year before, and sales professionals had targets they were measured against, but the process was far from robust, lacking any serious focus on planning for the employees' professional futures.

After a series of meet and greets in various regions, Justin did some investigation. He met with his counterpart in human resources, Marcus, who confirmed that the company didn't have anything close to a twenty-first-century succession-planning system, which Justin had been used to at his former job. Realizing that bolstering the firm's people processes was just as important as their sales and other administrative functions, Justin worked with Marcus to make the business case to the leadership team: designing a succession-planning system was the next logical step after the performance-management process, and it would facilitate the company's continued expansion into new markets.

The leadership team agreed. A project team was chartered, with Justin and Marcus as co-sponsors. Jennifer, an HR director in the corporate office, was appointed project manager, a stretch assignment that would test her ability to handle more responsibility. Her background was in compensation and benefits, so spearheading this new initiative would be a good supplement to her skill set. Courtney enthusiastically agreed to join the project team and provide a voice from the field, as did Rodney, an Atlanta-based store manager who had always been passionate about mentoring his people into advanced positions. Since the project team had been tasked with finding a technology-facilitated solution, they recruited Alex, corporate IT director, to round out the team.

The team got off to a strong start. They defined goals for the succession-planning system, established success criteria, and laid out a project plan. Jennifer did a great job of helping everyone get to know each other and share their hopes for the project.

Determining early on that they didn't have the requisite skills in-house, the team agreed to contract with a consulting firm to design the new succession-planning system. First, they laid out selection criteria. Next, they identified potential firms. Then, they requested a formal proposal from the three they felt best fit their needs.

After they received the proposals, it became clear that there were fundamental differences in the approaches and costs of the three vendors. The most expensive bid was from a global consulting firm with deep experience and a proven technology in succession planning. There was also a moderately priced bid from the firm that had worked with the company to implement its performance-evaluation system. While they were familiar with the company, there had been some issues with timeliness and quality of service, and it was unclear how well their succession-planning tool would actually work. The lowest bid came from a regional start-up firm that specialized in technology-facilitated human resource solutions, with a specialty in succession planning; it met all criteria the company was looking for. While small, this consulting firm had a solid list of several Fortune 500 clients and a reputation for having both great programmers as well as PhD-level psychologists on staff. They claimed to be able to facilitate a solid solution from both a technical and a people perspective.

Alex, the IT director, vociferously advocated for the high bidder, asserting that they had world-class support and the most clearly proven technical solution. Although the high bidder was costly, Alex argued that it was best to get it done right the first time.

Rodney, the store manager in Atlanta, expressed concerns that this vendor's tool might be too sophisticated for the folks in the field, who would need to participate in aspects of the process, such as the new online 360-degree feedback assessment (wherein subordinates, peers, and managers would provide developmental input for colleagues). Rodney felt the field reps were usually slow to adopt new technology.

Both he and Courtney were not in favor of working with the mid-priced vendor again; they'd both dealt with problems caused by the challenging implementation of the performance-management system. The two of them were instead enamored with several aspects of the low-priced firm's proposal. That consulting firm was the most flexible to deal with, customer service-oriented, eager for their business, and very willing to customize its software and process to make the interface extremely user-friendly for frontline staff.

Jennifer, the project manager, was aware of the problems the mid-priced vendor had created in the lower levels of the company during implementation of its performance-management system, but this consulting firm was extremely politically astute and had formed a collegial good old boy relationship with the firm's founder and current CEO. During golf outings and trips to the racetrack, the lead partner at the consulting firm had told the founder that his consultants had helped the company implement the performance-management system in spite of itself. Unfortunately, the founder believed him.

Behind the scenes, Jennifer canvassed the senior leaders she had access to and asked their opinion about the three proposals. Because they were in close proximity in the corporate office and because she knew most of them through her participation in discussions about executive compensation, this wasn't a terribly difficult task. Through her informal poll, she found that the majority favored the mid-priced vendor that had previously consulted on the performance-management process. The lead partner had ingratiated himself well, the firm was a known commodity, and it was a relatively cost-effective option.

Armed with that feedback, Jennifer furtively attempted to sway the group in the direction of the mid-priced vendor. However, when confronted with the sound arguments of her team members, she invariably backed down. As project manager, Jennifer was creative in trying to facilitate the team to reach a decision. She fostered an environment in which team members felt comfortable sharing their opinions—and they all did. Alex refused to budge from favoring the technically robust, high-priced vendor. Rodney strongly favored the highly customizable, low-priced option. Courtney continued to focus the group on the impact of each solution on those who would be involved in the process—such as ease of use, customer service response times, and unbiased information to help with personnel decisions. Yet, while originally siding with Rodney, she seemed to sway back and forth. She played devil's advocate for all three options, and it almost seemed to her teammates that she was trying to stir things up.

After three rounds of team meetings—in addition to information sessions with all three bidders—the team found itself at an impasse. Eventually they decided to lay the options before the leadership team, explain the pros and cons of each vendor, and ask them to make the final decision.

In the end, the leadership team selected the mid-priced vendor. While impressed with the global firm's capabilities, they didn't believe they needed that level of sophistication or that price tag. Of course, the most significant factor was the relationship between the founder and the vendor's lead partner. However, the leadership team was impressed by the start-up consulting firm and offered them a piece of the pie—namely, the company agreed to utilize the start-up vendor's on-staff psychologists to help coach participants through their 360-degree feedback results.

Implementation proved problematic. As suspected, the mid-priced vendor didn't have experience with several critical aspects of the succession-planning process, particularly in the areas of Web-based data collection and analysis. In the end, the start-up consulting firm was brought in for technical help in finalizing the design solution.

JUSTIN: THE ADAPTER EXECUTIVE

Although Justin had been successful at his previous employer, he'd been enticed to the new firm because he liked its fresh, innovative approach. Justin launched right into his new role as vice president, making many connections across the company and identifying the need for positive change. He looked beyond his role and saw how partnering with Marcus, his peer in HR, would help make the company's leadership pipeline stronger. Together they chartered a team to make it happen.

As he networked with his new colleagues, Justin heard rumblings that not everyone was impressed by the mid-priced vendor's past performance, and he became concerned. However, he chose to keep his reservations to himself. How much smoother would the process have been had Justin chosen to engage in challenging conversations with his peers on the leadership team instead of taking the comfortable, expedient path?

JENNIFER: THE ADAPTER PROJECT MANAGER

As project manager, Jennifer did a wonderful job launching the team: she provided goals and success criteria, set out a clear plan, and facilitated team building. Adapters like Jennifer excel at firing on all three cylinders—Head, Hands, and Heart. She was adept at involving people and facilitating compromise.

Jennifer brought several creative solutions to the table. It had been her idea to award part of the project to the start-up vendor. Over the course of the project she continued to develop relationships with that firm, and when the time came, she was able to convince the leadership team to bring them in to fix the mess caused by the main contractor.

However, she missed the opportunity to lead the project team away from the mid-priced vendor and correct the misperceptions the leadership team had about this vendor, and those proved to be costly missteps. While they can spark challenging debate, Adapter project managers like Jennifer can make their teams less than optimal in the decision-making department, thanks to the Adapter's discomfort with unpopular decisions.

COURTNEY: THE ADAPTER NEW SUPERVISOR

In the absence of a company-wide succession-planning system, Courtney invented and instituted some creative developmental forums in her own region, doing as much as her budget would allow. She involved her team members in quarterly half-day off-sites where they invited a speaker on a topic of interest, shared success stories, and featured a "rep roundtable" in which they would coach each other through thorny problems. Courtney's sales reps appreciated these activities. When asked to implement changes in her region, Courtney consistently did so in a participative fashion, using a flexible approach, invariably keeping herself open to new ideas.

Since she was at the target level in the organization, Courtney got to participate in the pilot implementation of the succession-planning process. As part of the 360-degree assessment, her direct reports and her manager were all requested to give her feedback using the new Web-based tool, and she was asked to select at least three peers to do so as well. She chose her fellow members on the succession-planning team. When she received her results, she saw that she'd been rated highly on many dimensions, but she was shocked to learn that some perceived her as "unpredictable" and "at times disruptive" to the process she was trying to support! As can be the case with Adapters, people at times found it difficult to relate to her or figure out where she was coming from.

The Adapter's Strengths

Justin, Courtney, and Jennifer are all Adapters. Adapters excel at identifying opportunities, crafting creative processes, and interacting with a wide variety of people. Adapters can be electric and magnetic, sparking creative ideas and magnetizing teams from a wide variety of backgrounds to make things happen.

Adapters model flexibility and openness to new approaches. New to the organization, Justin saw a gap, collected data about the problem, and engaged with others to fix it. Courtney, although inexperienced, sensed there was a better way and jumped at the chance to be part of the team that would find it. Jennifer rose to the challenge of solving an important business problem, laid out a solid plan that included objective decision-making criteria, and actively solicited a wide variety of input to reach a solution. In each case, the person showcased Heart, Head, and Hands in action.

The Adapter's Blind Spots

Yet, once again, any strength overdone can become a weakness. Adapters' flexibility can make it challenging for them to chart a strong course forward. Jennifer found herself swayed by the arguments of those around her, instead of articulating and supporting a position of her own. When soliciting the opinions of senior leaders, she hesitated to make the case that their favored vendor might not be the best choice given its past deficiencies. Similarly, Justin learned of the problems with the favored vendor but didn't introduce those concerns into the discussion. Courtney was surprised to learn how her team and peers at times found her unpredictable and that they were not always appreciative of her devil's advocate stance.

THE ADAPTER AS A LEADER

Most of the time you . . .

- Like to be personally involved and engaged with a wide variety of stakeholders in the change process—you are a very active and vocal change leader
- Are curious about what others think and feel, are open-minded, and consider the input of others
- Enjoy playing the role of a devil's advocate and challenging group assumptions or plans
- Like to experiment with different ways of doing things, thereby exhibiting flexibility and a willingness to adapt as you learn through the change process
- Show others that you are willing to compromise in order to overcome resistance or to convince others to take the first step in a new direction

But sometimes you . . .

- Can be so flexible that it can be difficult for you to determine which behaviors to deploy to reach your goals
- May at times value reaching an agreement above making a less-popular decision that makes better business sense (at least in the short term)
- Can be perceived as going around the chain of command when you work "behind the scenes" to achieve your objectives
- Can become bored by routine and tempted to stir things up to alleviate monotony
- Can be rigid or inflexible under pressure or when stressed

THE ADAPTER AS VIEWED BY OTHERS

Usually people see you as . . .

- Flexible
- Adaptable
- A team player
- Interactive
- Open to experimentation and new experience

However, occasionally you are . . .

- Unpredictable
- Political
- Wily
- Overly talkative
- Inconsistent in tasks and deliverables

The Adapter on the Job

Let's now take a deeper dive and look at how Adapters at all levels—executive, project management, and supervisory—can capitalize on their strengths and work on their weak spots.

THE ADAPTER AS A NEW SUPERVISOR

When asked to implement changes, Adapter new supervisors consistently do so in a participative fashion, using a flexible approach, and they are invariably open to new ideas. Yet, at times, people may find it difficult to relate to them or see where they're coming from.

Strengths of the Adapter New Supervisor

- You find it easy to build on your natural curiosity about what others think and feel, and to ask questions that enable you to help others adapt to change.
- You use your natural inventiveness to help others learn to flex their attitudes and behaviors to be more consistent with the change process.
- As you transition from team player to team leader, you help build a strong, cohesive group.

Traps Adapter New Supervisors Should Avoid

- When asked to implement changes that you suspect will be met with resistance, have you armed yourself with the information you need to adequately explain and perhaps defend management's position?
- When you encounter resistance, are you ever tempted to side with the resisters? If so, ask yourself: What do I really believe? What do I know is the right thing to do?

- In all instances, ask yourself: What are the implications for what I say and do for how I am perceived as a leader? For the success of the change initiative?

THE ADAPTER AS A PROJECT MANAGER

If you're an Adapter, you can typically get a project team off to a great start, establishing goals, delineating a project plan, and fostering team building. However, when your strengths at promoting compromise are overdone, your team can find itself lacking the will to make unpopular decisions.

Strengths of the Adapter Project Manager

- You find it easy to jump into a project leadership role, get to know the disparate players, help them get to know each other, and create a process for working together toward the goal.
- You can usually leverage your innate ability to connect with others to build a high-functioning team that's founded on solid ground rules.
- Given your inclination to interact broadly, you ensure that your team is not myopic and doesn't fall prey to groupthink, but instead actively canvasses for input, and listens to the concerns of key stakeholders outside the team.
- During challenging times in the change process, you devise creative solutions to get the group unstuck. You find another way to reach the goal and help people see things through a new lens.

Traps Adapter Project Managers Should Avoid

- You may find that maintaining your role as leader is a challenge—are you slipping back into the role of just another team member? Are you remaining resolute and holding the team to high standards of performance and decision making?

- When your team engages in challenging debates or confrontational behavior, are you able to facilitate the discussion and allow members to air dissenting opinions, or do you become uncomfortable if the discussion becomes heated (but professional) and attempt to snuff out the conflict? How can you become more tolerant of healthy conflict?

- How can you build your ability to facilitate conversations that eventually lead to consensus rather than settling for the quicker compromise?

- How can you consistently ensure that you are advocating for the right business decisions and not altering your position just because you want to maintain relationships (with team members, those in power, or others who you like or respect)? In those instances, ask yourself: What is the right path to take, and what will enable me to emerge as a respected leader?

THE ADAPTER AS AN EXECUTIVE

If you're an Adapter in an executive role, you have no doubt made broad connections and worked hard to identify the need for positive change. Your ability to drive meaningful, lasting change will be bolstered by more proactive willingness to engage in challenging conversations instead of making the comfortable, convenient choices.

Tips for Adapter Executives

- As executives, Adapters cast a wide net both in terms of people and ideas. You enjoy knowing and being known by a wide variety of people. Your curiosity keeps you apprised of the new and different, and you're keen to bring fresh ideas into your organization. You're

probably more comfortable in the limelight than your fellow executives, and you look for ways to capitalize on your penchant for interacting with others and emerge as an active and vocal change leader.

- Since you are naturally inquisitive, you have a unique ability to
  understand and articulate varying perspectives during a change
  process. You use this capacity to overcome tension, bridge gaps, and
  find common ground.
- You are open to the untested, and you're more willing than others
  to identify and invent novel ways of doing things. You help your
  organization embrace experimentation and reasonable risk taking so
  it continues to adapt and thrive into the future.

Traps Adapter Executives Should Avoid

- How can you rigorously test options to ensure they make business
  sense?
- How can you publically advocate for stances you believe in?
- In times of challenging change, can you ask a trusted colleague to
  help your team reach consensus rather than settling on the quickest
  compromise?

The Adapter: The Bottom Line

Adapters are role models for friendliness to change. When at their best,
they emerge as positive, engaging ambassadors for change.

In *The Leadership Challenge*, James Kouzes and Barry Posner list the five
pillars of great leaders, and one of them is a willingness to "Challenge the
Process." As the change leader style most open to experimentation, Adapters may be naturally inclined to do as Kouzes and Posner recommend and
"search for opportunities by seizing the initiative and exercising 'outsight,'

and experiment and take risks by generating small wins and learning from experience."[22]

Adapters generally help others do the same as well. Their natural inquisitiveness and change-friendliness increases the probability that they will create an environment in which people can arrive at insights themselves; and when people arrive at their own insights, they're much more likely to own the change. As David Rock and Jeffrey Schwartz write in their article "The Neuroscience of Leadership," "At a moment of insight, a complex set of new connections [in the brain] is being created. These connections have the potential to enhance our mental resources and overcome the brain's resistance to change. But to achieve this, given the brain's limited working memory, we need to make a deliberate effort to hardwire an insight by paying it repeated attention. That is why employees need to 'own' any kind of change initiative for it to be successful . . . For insights to be useful, they need to be generated from within, not given to individuals as conclusions."[23]

Adapters need to remember that flexibility and agreeableness are probably not the legacy they want to leave behind them as business leaders. Yes, great leaders need to consider the input of others and remain open to course corrections during times of change. But they also need to make unpopular decisions and keep moving forward confidently, with their compass pointed toward true north.

Self-assessment Questions

If you focus on Heart, Head, and Hands roughly equally as a change leader, ask yourself . . .

- Do people ever seem confused by you? Do they seem not to know how to take the things you say, or what to expect from you?
- Do you sometimes allow others to make expedient, comfortable choices instead of grounded, difficult business decisions?
- Do you find yourself changing opinions based on the people you are with at the moment, instead of remaining resolute in your own viewpoints?
- Do you at times find it challenging to firmly advocate for change when you encounter resistance from others, particularly from those you personally like or who are in positions of power?
- Do you question yourself about whether you're pursuing the right objectives, taking the right path, or following the right process?

 Visit www.ChangeCatalysts.com/BookResources for additional coaching hints on how Adapters can leverage their strengths and shore up their blind spots.

CHAPTER 11

NOW YOU KNOW YOUR CQ: WHAT'S NEXT?

Now that you know your change leader style—along with your strengths, blind spots, and the unique ways you contribute to an organization—where do you go from here?

The next step is to make sure that you keep working on your CQ. It's not enough to take the assessment, read the related chapter, and think you're done. You have to actually apply your new knowledge in day-to-day situations—to translate your insights into action! You have to constantly be aware of your style and look for productive ways to fill in the gaps you may be leaving open. In *First, Break All the Rules*, Marcus Buckingham and Curt Coffman argue that it's better to capitalize on our strengths rather than work on our deficits. While that may be true overall in our careers, in any given role we will each be tasked to be a change leader at some point, and for that, we need aspects of the Heart, Head, and Hands. If we ignore one of these three, we're drastically reducing our chances of success.

As you work on building your change intelligence, remember one subtle but important distinction: your goal is not to change yourself or your change leader style. Your goal is awareness and adaptation: becoming more aware of your tendencies, and honing your ability to adopt new behaviors when those would lead to more successful outcomes.

Regardless of your change leader style, here are two strategies to help you lead change intelligently and impactfully:

1. Design systems and structures to keep your blind spots on your radar screen. For example, if you are one of the low-Heart styles (a Driver, Executer, or Visionary), consider scheduling periodic process checks into team meetings to gauge what individuals are feeling and thinking. At an organizational level, consider periodic pulse checks, such as engagement surveys, to assess the impact of the change on the culture.

2. Partner with others who are strong where you are weak. For example, if you have a low Head score (Facilitators and some Coaches and Executers), include Visionaries, Champions, or Drivers on your project team. Or reach out to a Head-oriented business leader for feedback or mentoring.

*   *   *

I'm a Champion, and I love partnering with a wide variety of people in my client organizations to bring their visions to life. I get the big picture, and I enthusiastically work with people at all levels, in all functions, and within all disciplines to make it happen.

However, I know that I can get a lot more excited about the possibility of change and the promotion of the change than the details. I'm not a project manager, not the best one to "own" the project plan. I tend to find details boring, even though I realize how critical planning and follow-through are. Early in my career, I had many in-your-face opportunities to learn this lesson, both minor and major:

- I once arrived at an automotive plant at 7:00 a.m. to run a training session for several dozen people that started at 7:30. As soon as I walked in, I found that my co-facilitator, an internal consultant recently promoted from the machine shop, didn't have anything ready. My instructions had been to set up for the training session, but the poor person had never attended a nontechnical training session before, let alone organized one!

- I was once asked to return to a client organization to audit the status of the employee-engagement program we had designed only to find that the team had made no progress beyond continuing to meet monthly. While they had a great vision for the program on paper and an engaging communications plan drafted, they had no plan beyond that to roll the program out to the organization!

Since those early missteps, I've worked hard to address this weak link in my change leadership, and now that I've taken on that developmental challenge, one of my clients referred to me as "maniacally organized." It's not that I'm that way by nature; it's that I've learned that to be a successful change leader, I need to consciously add that missing ingredient to my recipe. When I do that, I'm able to successfully lead change that sticks.

In *What Got You Here Won't Get You There*, author Marshall Goldsmith notes, as he reflects on coaching leaders throughout his career, that "what's wrong is that they have no idea how their behavior is coming across to the people who matter—their bosses, colleagues, subordinates, customers and clients . . . My job is to help them see that the skills and habits that have taken them this far might not be the right skills and habits to take them further."[24]

This is true of people who rely on one aspect of change leadership to get them through any situation. Leading change through your dominant style may make you successful in the short term, but over time, you can greatly increase the probability of career success by attending to all three aspects of your change intelligence—the Heart, the Head, and the Hands.

So, now I remember to do structured project planning with action steps, deliverables, accountabilities, and time frames. I have checklists for setting up training sessions and meetings so that the details don't get dropped out. Looked at a different way, in my profession, as a change leadership consultant, my mission is to guide people toward their vision and engage them to work together toward the goal, to champion the change. As a Champion, I'm perfectly suited for that career path (if I do say so myself!). The skills I lack or don't enjoy using are the skills that my clients should use in their roles. They should be the Drivers and Facilitators and Executers of the change in their organizations. I receive high marks for my implementation skills. I love to roll up my sleeves, put on my hardhat and metatarsal boots and safety goggles and hearing protection, and make it real in the field. Yet, ultimately, my role is to let go, to let my clients own the plan and work the plan themselves.

Indeed, that's one of the reasons I created the CQ System—to provide clients a tangible, actionable assessment and a supporting toolkit to help them start building their talents as change leaders right away. I wanted to give people not just the *what* and *why* but the *how*, too.

Now that you've diagnosed your CQ and taken the first steps toward an action plan for developing your change intelligence, you're ready to move past the individual level. In the next section of the book, you'll find out how CQ can help teams and organizations lead powerful change.

But before you leave this section, don't forget to study the change leader styles close to yours. For example, if you are a Visionary (more Head-oriented) but your Heart score indicates that you are pretty close to the Champion (blend of Head and Heart) style, check out that chapter as well for insights and hints that may help you.

PART III
APPLYING CQ

In Part III, you transition from learning about your personal CQ to CQ in wider contexts. Just as developing change intelligence is a critical competency for individual change leaders, so is it a core competency to bake into the DNA for teams and organizations.

Chapter 12 looks at how three teams utilized the CQ System to build their capacity to jointly lead change. Then, in chapter 13, we broaden the scope to CQ at the organizational level and study how three firms facing very different change challenges built change intelligence across levels to meet them.

In chapter 14, you'll find guidance on navigating the phases of the change lifecycle—moving from *planning* to *doing* to *sustaining*. Finally, in chapter 15, you'll learn strategies for moving people through the various phases of human reactions to change—from *denial* to *resistance* to *exploration* to *commitment*.

CHAPTER 12

CQ FOR TEAMS

You've seen how understanding and growing CQ can help individuals at every level of an organization. Like individuals, teams have their own degrees of change intelligence and their own distinctive change styles. These arise naturally from the compilation of the team's individual members, and the team takes on a dimension of its own. Like humans, teams are distinct entities made up of unique cognitive, affective, and behavioral characteristics. And beyond the simple sum of the three dimensions, many team dynamics can be explained through what emerges when the individual styles come together in the mix.

Following are examples of how CQ has helped real teams get real results.

CQ for a Project Launch

The first team-based case study involves a manufacturing firm whose business is cyclical, with lots more sales in the summer. To meet this demand, the company—a family-owned business that had been operating for decades—would hire hundreds of temporary workers for several months in the winter to produce and ship inventory. Although this had been the pattern since the company's founding, no one had ever established a wholly satisfactory system for training these temporary workers. To change that, the company hired Will as its new training manager and asked him to put together a team that would get the job done.

Will and his team had their work cut out for them. The company was cutting costs everywhere and struggling to schedule even basic compliance training around their workloads. Plus, the team would need the help of supervisors during their busiest season and the cooperation of full-time frontline employees who generally viewed temps as a nuisance.

One of the first things Will did was to bring me in to conduct a change leadership workshop for the new team. The firm had a history of resisting innovation, particularly when it was introduced by outsiders or new managers. "We'll outlast the new guy," the jaded senior employees would say. "We'll smile and nod at 'his way,' then after he moves on, we'll get back to running things our way." The mentality was program-of-the-year personified!

The initial workshop focused on the CQ System. Each team member completed the CQ/Change Intelligence Assessment, and then, during one of the first project team meetings, they shared their results. The scores indicated that this was a Heart-oriented team with a dominant Coach profile. The ensuing discussion highlighted the following positive findings, all revealing the team's Heart focus:

- "We are a family-oriented firm. We really do talk to our people one-on-one and listen to their concerns."
- "Each supervisor holds team meetings where we try to involve our people, explain to them what is going on, and show what's in it for them."
- "People know they can talk to management about anything—from their direct boss to the owner."

They had affirmed the company's people-centered approach, but they wondered if that could be a weakness, too. Indeed it could. At times the team found it impossible to incorporate everyone's opinions, and difficult changes didn't get implemented. Caring at times devolved into coddling, leading to low accountability and avoidance of confrontation, even when negative behaviors stood in the way of necessary improvements. And everyone having the owner's ear meant that members could bypass frontline leadership, albeit with the best of intentions.

Moving from strengths to blind spots, the team was struck by several observations:

- "We have only one Driver. No wonder we never get anything done!" (This showed a Hands weakness.)
- "We have no Executers. No wonder we don't have anything resembling a plan yet!" (This too showed a Hands weakness.)
- "We only have a few people who focus on the 'what and why' from a business sense. No wonder we can't get resources from the executive team!" (This showed a Head weakness.)

Indeed, the team had only a limited number of people with a strong Hands orientation. While some demonstrated a moderate tendency toward the Hands, it was certainly no one's strength. In their first meeting, one team member complained that the team wasn't even necessary, because they already had a lot of training materials for the winter temps, but they had never been used as intended. Another commented that Will was the first manager at the firm who had a project management certification and that it showed by how poorly projects were typically managed. Others pointed out that project teams in the operational side of the house, like this one, had historically struggled to communicate with the senior leaders who chartered them, leading to frustration and a feeling that the two groups spoke different languages. "We talk about the people," one person said, "but they just want to hear about the bottom line."

Through the CQ System, the team had a way to discuss, explain, and deal with these tendencies—and to aim for a better outcome in the future. As a team they agreed to the following:

- We need to maintain our strength of open and frequent one-on-one and group communication (leveraging the Coach).
- However, we need to right the balance between caring and listening and asserting and challenging (improving Visionary and Driver skills).
- We need to make a project plan, assign accountabilities and time frames, and review these frequently (acting more like Executers).
- We must ensure that each team member's manager is informed and aligned with the team's purpose and plan (building up Driver behaviors).
- We need to arrange for periodic meetings with the sponsoring executives and interact with them in a way that demonstrates the team's business savvy and grasp of key success factors—not only from a training and employee-engagement perspective, but also from a bottom-line business perspective (acting more like Visionaries).
- We need to make a point of demonstrating meaningful successes targeted to specific groups along the way, which may be different for the frontline employees, supervisors, and executives (acting more like Champions).

Armed with these insights and agreements, the team set itself up to achieve real results. They linked the operational and technical bench strength they were building through the training program to another initiative that was at the top of company executives' minds—namely, acquiring a new manufacturing facility. Integrating the new facility meant that several of the most highly talented supervisors and operators would need to spend months transitioning their systems to comply with the parent firm's. Therefore, in their absence, employees at the existing plant would need to run the business without reliance on those highly skilled and experienced colleagues for a period of time. The training was essential to equipping other supervisors and operators to step up to the challenge.

The team also partnered with the company's finance group to track metrics that would help them build a business case for the training budget. With that work done, they were able to speak the business language of the executives. To bring it all together, the team relied on Will, with his project management background, to draft a project plan and keep them on track. After a year, the team had revamped the company's training system: they'd designed a system with roles for executive sponsors, supervisor participation, and training team oversight; developed training programs for twenty jobs across five production lines; incorporated training scorecards with key performance indicators; and trained over two hundred new employees and over a hundred tenured employees.

CQ for Departmental Team Building

In addition to guiding the creation of a project team, an understanding of CQ can also help revamp and improve an existing departmental team. The group in the next case study had worked together for two years, and its members were already reasonably well acclimated to each other. They worked for a firm in the recruitment industry, and the team members were all masters-level industrial-organizational psychologists, and were thus highly skilled and experienced in a wide variety of assessment tools. They had been through a battery themselves, both on the job and during their studies.

Though headed by a competent director and made up entirely of manager-level personnel, the team was a collection of people in their mid-twenties to early thirties, who were relatively early in their careers. Moreover, the company was going through massive change—it was penetrating new global markets and launching new products and services at a dizzying rate. Several of these new initiatives—including a new online survey and new reporting metrics—were assigned to the team, which would have to design and execute them.

Carmen, the director of the team, decided to conduct a team-building event highlighting the CQ System. It would, she hoped, help the team navigate all these changes and emerge as a stronger group.

Each individual took the CQ/Change Intelligence Assessment, and then the group met to share results. Being a fun, lively, open group, they decided to make a game out of it: they all tried to guess each other's style. They got each one correct. Each of the seven team members had a different change leader style—there was one of each in the group—meaning that the combined team profile was that of an Adapter.

The team made the following observations during the session:

- "We know each other so well that we could guess each other's styles. That's validating."
- "We have a good mix of styles. We know who has different strengths and can rely on them when we need to."
- "With all the changes going on at this company, it's important for our team to be Adapters—so this is a good profile for us to have collectively. Our team needs to constantly turn on a dime."

This was also a high-functioning, open team, and the members were able to give and receive challenging feedback to each other based on the results of the assessment. This feedback invariably came from a place of honesty and continuous improvement.

- "That you're an Executer is great for our team and for me, since as a Visionary I am so much more a big-picture person. But sometimes I do think you lose sight of where we're going and can get too wrapped up in minor tasks that in the end don't add much value."

- "I appreciate always knowing where you're coming from [as a Driver]. You don't mince words and are always confident in your opinions. That said, I wish you could be a little more open-minded when I come to you with a different approach, even though I might not have done all the research to back it up yet."

- "I think it's great that our director is a Coach. I do feel I can always come to you. You listen, and I know you care about my development. But sometimes in meetings with the vice president, it seems a stronger style would work better. Sometimes it would be good to see you push back on things that don't make sense and cause us to have to rework things we spent weeks designing. Often, the VP's reasons don't sound all that good—it seems like he's just being capricious."

In the end, the team emerged with new insights about themselves, fresh respect for each other, and agreements on how to work together—and with others outside the team—in more powerful ways.

CQ for the Senior Team in Strife

Senior teams, too, can reap great rewards from a look at their collective CQ, especially when they find themselves in a rough spot. One cross-functional team of executives from different units in a pharmaceutical organization I worked with had been charged with sponsoring the implementation of new financial planning and tracking software. The project wasn't going well at all. The IT group within the pharmaceutical company was frustrated with the technology vendor because of all the undocumented problems with the new software release. The technology firm was frustrated with the pharmaceutical company for frequently changing its requirements. The business leaders within the pharmaceutical firm were frustrated with lack of technical support for the process of defining requirements and designing the solution.

Grossly behind schedule and well over budget, the technology vendor suggested using the CQ System as a way to initiate and focus discussion about the current state of the project. Representatives from the vendor hoped this step would promote nondefensive dialogue and point to a way forward. Team members at the pharmaceutical company agreed, and each team member took the CQ/Change Intelligence Assessment. When they met to share the results, they found that the team had a very high Head score, with the overall change leader style of the Driver.

Although the team's dominant profile was that of the Driver, it had a bimodal distribution, with three Visionaries and two Executers (in addition to an Adapter who was close to the Executer style). This meant that the team's biggest weakness was Heart. Collectively, the members were frustrated by their inability to drive forward and make swift progress toward their objective. But the results offered an enlightening window into the dysfunctional dynamics of the project:

- "We have too few Heart people—no wonder we never came together as a team and don't communicate effectively."
- "No wonder we don't meet our goals. The only Executers are the external project managers, and they have no power to get things done inside the organization. The rest of us have our day jobs, and we haven't had our eye on the prize."
- "No wonder the business leaders are constantly changing their requirements—they're all Visionaries. And we [the technical vendor], with our focus on the design work, haven't given them the training to really appreciate the implications of what they are asking for."

Moreover, the results and ensuing conversation paved the way for positive new agreements. For the first time, this group was feeling like a real team.

- "We need to implement hour-long, weekly project team meetings" (to focus on the Heart).

- "We need to integrate certain accountabilities into each executive's personal goals" (to spread the Hands orientation).
- "We should conduct a training workshop for the business owners, to show them how to use the new technology" (to add a Facilitator focus).
- "We need to devote an internal technical person to interface between the technology department, business owners, and the technology vendor" (to bolster the Champion and Driver behaviors).
- "We need to assign an executive-level sponsor from the technology vendor to the team, and he or she needs to ensure that the company is kept up-to-date on any best practices learned while implementing the new release. Basically, this vendor has got to have more skin in the game" (to Champion and Drive alignment).

This project is still a work in progress, but the CQ System provided an opening for the team to come together for the first time. In a safe forum, they hashed out what was working, what wasn't, and why. Aligning themselves and settling on new agreements enabled the senior team to finally nail down the business requirements and understand how to provide sufficient technical support. The pharmaceutical firm got what it needed from the software, and the vendor learned a great deal they were able to leverage during future engagements with other clients.

The Most Common Question about CQ for Teams

Most of my clients ask me the same question, and it's a good one: "What blend of change leader styles is best to have on a team? Is there an ideal team profile?"

In the short term, a particular team profile may be most appropriate to address a specific need. A Driver team would be invaluable for a high-intensity, make-it-or-break-it turnaround. A Champion team would be particularly adept at rallying an organization around a radically new vision. A Facilitator team would be of great assistance in implementing a complex new technology on the front lines.

Just as there is no ideal individual profile, there is ultimately no ideal team profile. Success lies not in the numerical results or your position on the CQ triangle, but rather in how aware the team is of its CQ results and what it does to address them. Just as the best change leaders are enlightened by knowledge of their style, their strengths, and their blind spots, so it is for the ideal team.

My longest-standing co-facilitator and I are the opposite styles. I'm a Champion, and he's an Executer. When we first met, it was like we were speaking two different languages, and I couldn't get where he was coming from half the time. However, we both trusted and respected each other. As we learned each other's styles, we began to value and appreciate what each other brought to the table.

Over the years, the two of us have led many change projects together. Invariably, he owns the project plan—and mercifully so! His spreadsheets boast multiple worksheets, many tabs, and an abundance of color. Every *i* dotted and *t* crossed. I, on the other hand, tend to take the lead with facilitating project meetings. That said, his more detail-oriented and unemotional style can play better with technically oriented types. We are each a good balance to the other. Clients get the benefit of both our styles, our different perspectives and provocative viewpoints, and our complementary skill sets. We each add a lot of value as individuals, and we make an even more powerful team by knowing, acknowledging, and leveraging our collective strengths. It's not necessarily that Champions and Executers are natural-born partners; the benefit comes from my co-facilitator and I exploring our own brand of change intelligence and using our awareness of each other's predispositions and working styles to collaborate effectively.

The Biggest Danger of Team CQ

One caveat as you apply CQ to your team: Be sure that you don't dump all responsibility on certain individuals because the work seems suited to their CQ style. Don't assume that just because you're the Visionary, you'll always own the strategy. Don't assume that because you're the Coach, all the people dynamics fall on your plate. Don't dump all the minutiae of project planning on the Executer or have the Champion make all the executive presentations. Don't expect the Facilitator to run every team meeting or the Driver to kick butt and take names when things go awry. That's stereotyping. We each have a profile, but "profiling" is forbidden!

The CQ System is a tool, and just like a knife, it can be used as a utensil or as a weapon. The most effective teams use CQ to cut through the stuff that's holding its members back, not to cut members down by devaluing their style, or cut them off from contributing in ways that may be less common for their style.

In one steel mill I consulted with, I was working with the management team in the metallurgical department. Five of the six members had similar profiles—there were five Drivers (including one with Visionary tendencies and another with Executer tendencies). The outlier was a Facilitator who was right on the Coach border—and also the only woman and the only black person on the team.

The session was very moving. The team talked about how they had initially devalued this Facilitator's contributions because she seemed "soft" and too focused on "the fluffy, people details." They thought she spent far too much time training the new hires and not enough time getting them to do productive work. However, after the company only narrowly averted a union drive, her peers realized that she was actually the only one on the team who was listening to the staff's needs and concerns, and who understood their confusion over how things worked, as was the case during a recent clash over the bonus system. The team came to appreciate her unique perspective and her gift for connecting with people and inventing creative work processes that got the job done in a way that was palatable to the technicians. In the end, the management team realized that while she may have been less likely to focus on company-wide strategy and more apt to want to move the group at a more moderate pace, she was a major asset to the team.

Applying CQ to Your Team

Teams charged with leading change together can reap great benefits from exploring their collective change intelligence. Here are some questions to spark dialogue and new working agreements for future success.

1. What is our team's value to the organization, particularly with respect to leading change?

2. Is our team operating as effectively as it could be?

3. If not, why not? Can a deficit of CQ explain any of these reasons?

4. How can we apply our knowledge of CQ to improve our team's effectiveness?

5. How are we leading change effectively? What are the positive things happening in our current change project?

6. How can the CQ System help us understand the ways we aren't leading change effectively? What are the negative aspects of our current change project?

7. Is there a previous change project we can learn from—one we can dissect and interpret in light of what we now know about CQ? Can we create agreements among the team based on these insights and then carry them forth into the future?

8. What is our team's overall change leader style? Given that, at what

aspects of leading change do we predict our team will excel? What are our team's strengths?

9. What aspect of CQ (Heart, Head, or Hands) is our team lowest in? Which team member (or members) provides a complementary perspective that can help the team overcome its blind spots? What contributions can specific team members make to increase the effectiveness and positive impact of the team's actions?

10. Taken together, what are action steps for us to build our CQ as a team to lead powerful, positive change?

By the end of this discussion, the team will have reached a consensus on how to improve relationships and roles within the team and will have made new agreements on how best to enhance processes and results. Continue the process at future meetings by applying the chapters to follow on "CQ and the Stages of the Change Lifecycle" as well as "CQ and Phases of Human Reactions to Change"; that is, by selecting the right tools at the right time from the change management toolkit to help your team move the change process forward.

Periodically, bring the team back together to review its progress, make any necessary course corrections, and celebrate its successes!

 Visit www.ChangeCatalysts.com/BookResources for tips for facilitating an initial CQ-based session and how to handle common participant questions.

CHAPTER 13

CQ FOR ORGANIZATIONS

We've seen that individuals and teams have a change style and level of change intelligence, and CQ is also a component of every organization's culture. Some companies thrive on change, responding deftly to new economies, technologies, and customer expectations, while others are slow to adapt, and still others fail to change effectively and thus die.

Unfortunately, most companies fall into the latter two categories. Why do most organizations fail to achieve their lofty transformational goals? Often, it's because one or more of these is the case:

- Change is not championed by leaders high enough in the organization.
- The new change is led just the same way the last change was (which probably failed or was less than stellar).
- There is no consistent approach to change. At best, there are pockets of "strategic planning" or "change management" methodologies sprinkled throughout the organization—perhaps a project management methodology used in IT, or a change management model touted by human resources—but they are not endorsed or deployed company-wide.

- Leaders are not trained in change leadership. At best, they may have attended a class in change management, but they have had no opportunity to understand or develop their competency as change leaders. When change happens, they're under fire and have no time for reflection or coaching.
- Leaders lack awareness about what encourages people to embrace change, making it almost impossible to adapt to the needs of various audiences, lessening the probability that those stakeholders will get in action consistent with the change.
- Resistance is ignored or perceived as a force to be overcome. The focus is on doing something *to* the resisters, not *with* or *for* them, even when they can potentially provide valuable perspectives. Resistance continues, expands, and ultimately derails the change process.

Sound familiar? When you look at the last change project you were involved in, can you see one or more of these dynamics at work? In isolation or in combination, they are the death knell for a multitude of major change initiatives. When these projects fail, the investment is wasted, employee cynicism grows, and loyalty and trust are eroded.

Just as for individuals and teams, an organization's CQ can grow over time. Individuals can become more powerful change leaders through diagnosing and developing their own CQ, and teams can become more impactful in leading a change initiative through a CQ-based team-building experience. In the same way, the more CQ is infused into an organization—layered up, down, and across it—the more positive, predictable, and pervasive the company's results will be.

CQ at the organizational level isn't an add-on program, another task to complete, or another box to check. Rather, it is a model and mindset that empowers individuals, teams, and organizations to fundamentally alter the way they lead any kind of change initiative. When deployed effectively, the CQ approach becomes "how we do change in this organization," not just an appendage that's sometimes used and sometimes isn't. Companies that use the CQ System in this way find that it becomes a common language and a compass that points the way toward promising new outcomes.

Once members of an organization understand that they need to inspire the Heart, engage the Head, and help the Hands in each and every change initiative, they can employ a variety of other tools to heighten their change intelligence. Are executives *committed to sponsoring* the change? Perhaps a Leadership Alignment tool can help (to inspire the Heart). Are managers *aware* of the change and *informed* sufficiently so they can cascade the message to the troops? Perhaps they can utilize communication-planning methodologies (to engage the Head). Are frontline employees *trained* to use the new technology? Supervisors can deploy a learning plan (to help the Hands). In this way, CQ enables appropriate integration of methodologies from a variety of disciplines, spanning from change management to project planning and beyond.

Without an understanding of CQ, these types of tools are often deployed slavishly, to every project, whether they are needed or not. Or they are not used at all or not at the right time or in the right ways. Knowledge of CQ alerts leaders to when and how these supplemental approaches may make a positive difference. Furthermore, once a common toolkit of methodologies is installed across the system, everyone—from executives to the front line—will be singing off the same sheet of music, so to speak. No longer will helpful tools be used haphazardly; instead, everyone will be working in clearly understood and consistent ways to make the change come to life.

To paraphrase a TV commercial, CQ doesn't do change, it helps you do change better. The CQ System helps leaders integrate additional tools at the right time in the right way to ensure that everyone is on the same productive path toward real organizational change.

Can Your Organization Benefit from the CQ System?

No matter how successful your company is, chances are you can improve it further by building your collective CQ. Let's look at how pressing your organization's need for more change intelligence is.

Your organization might especially benefit from CQ if...

- Change seems hard; there is resistance to change (or, what looks like resistance); and people seem "change-fatigued," tired of the stress of constant change.
- Your leaders struggle to manage change; your leaders lack confidence.
- Change initiatives are typically suboptimal, or often fail outright.
- People complain about the "program of the year;" changes fail to stick, and improvements don't last over the long term.
- You lack a consistent, organization-wide approach to leading change; you find that different pockets in your organization use different methodologies—or none at all.

Let's now look at how CQ has helped three organizations in diverse industries transform their cultures to ones that embrace and thrive on change. As you read these case studies, notice precisely how the company overcame or avoided the factors that threatened to derail the change initiative. Also, note how its leaders integrated CQ with other change management methodologies and tools, enabling them to lead change more effectively, get better results, and build their organizations' overall level of change intelligence.

CQ Guides a Full-Asset Merger

The first case study involves a healthcare system, the largest in a highly competitive market. After a recent forced acquisition, the hospital brought on a new facility and expanded from four hundred to over six hundred beds. Now the leadership team was faced with the opportunity to follow up this successful acquisition with a full-asset merger.

The CEO wanted to use the CQ System to take the pulse of his leadership team before they took on this change challenge. The CQ process gave the team a common language to talk about the rifts within their team. As is not uncommon in healthcare systems, there was a division between the clinical staff, who were more apt to focus on the needs of patients and their families, and the administrative staff, who cared about the populations they served but who were more apt to stress fiscal realities.

Of the administrators, the CEO and COO were Champions, and the director of finance was a Driver. All three had high Head scores. Of the clinical staff, the chief medical officer and director of Child Services were Coaches, and the chief nursing officer and director of Critical Care were Facilitators. All four clinicians had high Heart scores.

Upon receiving their CQ results, the team members saw that their differences were not simply the result of their different roles, but also of their different tendencies as change leaders. Not only did they have fundamental differences in their decision-making criteria, they also approached change management in very dissimilar ways. These differences were being brought to the fore by the pressing requirements of the asset merger.

As their consultant, I saw the opportunity to further bolster the organization's change intelligence by introducing the concept of the organizational lifecycle, a supplemental model to CQ that I felt would educate the team at an even deeper level about their system's current state and its future. I facilitated a dialogue about how the healthcare system, due in part to the recent acquisition, was transitioning from its entrepreneurial roots to a new form that would require new systems and procedures. I observed that this was proving to be a frustrating transition for many, and they agreed. The clinical staff bemoaned what they perceived as a move toward stifling bureaucracy. Conversely, the administrative staff saw the lack of consistency across facilities as making the organization less efficient and successful than it might be with appropriate processes and controls in place.

As a result of this conversation, the members of the leadership team began to appreciate the fact that their rifts were the result of honest differences of opinion that were in turn (at least in part) the result of their personal change leader styles. Moreover, they saw that the friction they were experiencing was a normal—and even healthy—indication of where their system was in the organizational lifecycle. I used an analogy these healers were familiar with: in the human body, pain is uncomfortable, but it also signals that something is wrong. Likewise, conflict on a team indicates that there is a deeper problem in need of attention.

Armed with this new knowledge, the leadership team was able to craft a plan for the full-asset merger that deftly balanced the need for flexibility and commonality. Being a strong Driver, the director of finance took on the job of drafting the project plan, assigning accountabilities to his fellow executives as appropriate.

Next, the leadership team recognized that to make the plan a reality, they needed the active participation of all levels in the system. They also recognized that the tone they had set at the top—that is, of conflict between clinical staff and their administration peers—had parallels throughout the organization. This had historically led to challenges in implementing new procedures, and with the even more fundamental changes in day-to-day operations that were mandated by the merger, the leadership team realized it needed to make a concerted effort to transform this divisive dynamic.

So, to enable middle and frontline managers to partner with executives, transform the culture, and implement the new work practices, the leadership team cascaded the CQ System throughout the ranks. They made sure that the change plan incorporated methods and messages that connected with people's Hearts, Heads, and Hands, and that it helped traditionally siloed groups appreciate each other and work together in new ways, no matter what level of the system they operated at.

The chief nursing officer, a strong Facilitator, was particularly passionate about training and empowering nurses to lead change more effectively. Her nursing leaders continually bemoaned the fact that they felt wedged between the very legitimate issues of their staff nurses, the challenging relationships they had with some of their physicians, and what appeared to be a lack of empathy from administration. Many of the nursing leaders struggled to explain the *why* of the changes to their nurses and found themselves unable to adequately address the nurses' concerns about overload and stress. The chief nursing officer agreed to draft and own a learning plan that included all staff at all levels. The plan would help the leadership team develop their staff so that each person could take on his or her own responsibilities in the transition. Importantly, learning events would incorporate upward feedback, so the leadership team could understand and address the issues people were experiencing during the change, within and across departments.

After the first year, the newly integrated hospital had transformed from losing money to making a profit, a significant financial turnaround that was poised to continue through the enhanced efficiencies realized through the full asset merger. Both anecdotal data and employee-engagement survey results indicated increases in teamwork across the healthcare system, with the greatest improvements occurring in the nursing group.

CQ Transforms a National Retail Chain

The CQ System also helped a national retail organization with over two thousand full-service and specialty stores across the United States as it sought a more consistent approach to managing change across its many geographically dispersed locations. The company was constantly rolling out new initiatives—new products, services, customer relations protocols, human resource policies, technologies, and so on. Tales from the field indicated a great deal of variability in how people understood, adopted, and applied these new methods. Thus, company leaders decided to pilot a new approach to managing change.

Five years prior to this decision, company leaders had embarked on a new approach to attracting and developing high-potential technical talent. The goal of the High-potential Information Technology Leader (HIT) program was to win the company a return on its enormous investment in technology by developing leaders who had a keen grasp on emerging technologies and how they could be applied in a large retail organization. The HIT program brought in masters-level IT grads from top programs, each with five to ten years of work experience.

Members of the HIT program spent two years working in various business units, participating in monthly group training sessions, assisting in leading strategic business and technology initiatives, and receiving coaching from senior company leaders. At the conclusion of their program, participants were placed in a permanent position in one of the company's locations. Thereby, the company hoped to plant many seeds across its dispersed operations.

Five years after the HIT program began, company leaders reasoned that this group of fresh, young leaders would be the perfect vehicle for launching their new approach to leading change. Therefore, the CQ System was integrated into the program's leadership development curriculum.

The CQ System is powerful alone and even more powerful when paired with a solid change management and project-planning methodology. On the IT side of this retail company, major technology implementations and upgrades had suffered due to a lack of structured project management. Therefore, as a first step the HIT program leaders studied and selected generic approaches to change management and project management and then molded them into company-customized methodologies and tools.

Next, some members of the HIT program—company leaders and those responsible for grooming the new leaders in the field—participated in CQ sessions themselves. Then we worked together to incorporate the CQ System into the HIT program's monthly group training sessions.

HIT program participants were asked to apply the project management, change management, and change leadership/CQ tools to the various projects they spearheaded. During their monthly meetings, they gave and received feedback about their successes with applying the tools, and shared their struggles with moving people in positive new directions. Peers coached each other and provided insights. Managers engaged in similar conversations during their monthly one-on-one coaching sessions.

In one particularly telling but not uncommon example, a participant named Jared explained that store managers in his region said they supported a new process for fulfilling special orders from other stores—but he felt like it was just lip service. These managers were doing little if anything on a daily basis to engage their teams in adopting the new process. Jared's peers in the program helped him see that his approach to leading change left something to be desired: he'd been sending emails to store managers about the new process and attaching quick reference guides to be used as training material. They suggested that Jared visit the stores, meet personally with the managers and associates, and conduct live training and question-and-answer sessions on the benefits of the new process and how to use it.

Jared took their advice. At the next meeting, he reported that the stores in his region had welcomed his personal involvement. To his surprise, he got feedback on a few design flaws that made the process difficult for users, and he'd been able to fix these problems relatively quickly. Jared still had some work to do, but adoption in his region increased dramatically, and the technology was enhanced for deployment to other regions through the detailed end-user input. Moreover, Jared became a staunch advocate for utilizing communication and learning plans as integral parts of new technology-implementation projects.

Results of the initiative overall were compelling. ROI for new technology installations improved significantly. The integrated PM/CM/CQ toolkit is now widely dispersed and utilized throughout the organization.

CQ Develops Leaders at a Steel Company

CQ also came to the aid of a steel producer that had started up in the mid-nineties as a mini-mill. Like all mini-mills, it was designed to compete with large, integrated steel producers by adopting a lean approach to its operations and its human resource practices. Though it was financially successful, the firm struggled on several fronts. When the founding CEO announced his retirement, the firm realized it had not paid sufficient attention to developing its leadership pipeline. As is typical in many industries, front-line leaders were promoted into their first supervisory positions with no training beyond the basic human resource responsibilities of managers. The firm's value as a low-cost producer translated into minimal internal spending, which in turn meant that leaders at all levels received scant training.

There were many indications that this approach needed to be altered. General managers leading six-hundred-person facilities were forced to personally intervene in petty scuffles between operations and maintenance supervisors. Instead of professionally managing conflicts between their departments, customer service and mill managers would get into public screaming matches. Basically, all levels of management were operating at least one or two levels below what their job titles would suggest. Neither they nor those below them understood how to manage any differently.

Such dynamics are not uncommon in manufacturing facilities purporting to operate under a lean philosophy. When they brought me on board as their consultant, I helped them learn a lesson from Roger Herman and Joyce Gioia's book, *Lean and Meaningful*: perhaps counterintuitively, effective lean operations require an even greater focus on the human side of business. Without stifling layers of management and bureaucracy, every individual in the organization needs to be a leader. And, given frequently changing market conditions, customer requirements, and regulations—many of which resulted in changes to work procedures—every leader needed to have a high CQ to help his or her team adapt. To stay lean and continually adaptive, the organization as a whole needed to put systems in place to ensure that change was happening intelligently and sustainably.

Indeed, as a study[25] of thirty steel mills found, investment in positive human resource practices (as opposed to a "command and control" management style) directly correlates with bottom-line benefits in uptime and yield, two key metrics in the steel industry. HR practices such as inviting participation in problem solving (inspiring the Heart), sharing information broadly (engaging the Head), and providing adequate training (helping the Hands) were all approaches that equipped people for working together toward positive change.

These insights about the industry-specific, bottom-line benefits of building CQ caused the leadership team to turn the mirror inward toward itself. The leadership team decided it would start at the top, and those at the highest two levels of the organization underwent a 360-degree feedback process and completed self-assessments of their leadership competencies.

Three main findings came out of this process: leaders at the firm did not consistently (1) manage change effectively; (2) manage their own emotional reactions and relationships with others in a professional manner; or (3) provide sufficient feedback, coaching, or developmental opportunities to their staff.

Based on these results, the team agreed to embark on a leadership development program, starting with itself. The program would then cascade down to department heads, and finally to frontline supervisors. It would consist of multiple group sessions focusing on each of the team's weak spots. In between the sessions, which would be spaced three months apart, the executives would complete "action learning assignments" to apply and practice the skills they learned in the sessions, engage in peer coaching and accountability calls, and receive personalized help from a professional coach.

The leadership team used the CQ System to help improve its change management capacity. As a supplement that would help them manage their emotions and relationships more effectively, I introduced the team to emotional intelligence (EQ) concepts and tools. Introducing the concept of EQ to steel executives prompted everything from eye rolls to—to put it mildly—extreme antagonism. "We don't do that touchy-feely crap," some said. "What's next, a team hug and 'Kumbaya'?" I explained that according to a study,[26] when employees received EQ training, injuries and accidents were reduced by over 40 percent—and that got them listening. The company had just suffered a fatality, so reducing accidents was a sensitive and important matter. They still didn't understand EQ, but they were curious to learn more, assuming it could really have such a dramatic impact.

I also explained the benefits other EQ studies had revealed: that through enhancing employees' and leaders' self-awareness and self-management, as well as social awareness and relationship management, companies saw dramatic improvements in cost savings, quality, and customer satisfaction. Since the firm was constantly undergoing change initiatives in all these areas and more—many of which resulted in disappointing outcomes due to lack of consistent and effectual change leadership—light bulbs started turning on.

In this same initial session, participants did a peer-coaching exercise originated by Marshall Goldsmith in *What Got You Here Won't Get You There*. His "feedforward" exercise involves each participant identifying a behavior they wanted to change, and soliciting ideas from other participants one-on-one as to what they might try to improve. Unbelievably, for some, this was the first time they had received peer input on their own development in their twenty-plus-year careers.

One of the younger executives, the general manager of a recently acquired mill, requested feedback about how to inspire his employees as he communicated with them about change. An engineer by training, he typically announced an impending change in a staff meeting with his direct reports and expected them to carry the message forward. In a recent example, this GM had informed his staff that one of their product lines was being shifted to a sister mill, which would result in changes to production and scheduling. To his surprise, a few days later he started hearing rumors that employees were afraid the mill would be shut down. There was even speculation that the new parent company had purchased them just to reduce competition and transfer all their business to its other facilities. Initially, the GM ignored this, discounting the rumblings as the product of the typical rumor mill. Yet, when he learned that their best rolling mill operator was quitting because he felt he didn't have job security and that many other top workers were applying to the new automotive plant being built in the next town, he started paying attention. Maybe, as a leader, there was something he could do differently.

This GM got many viable suggestions from his peers. They proposed that he run town hall meetings and share messages directly with the front line; that he provide his staff with talking points to help them communicate easy-to-misinterpret messages; and that he invite corporate executives and GMs from other mills to visit his plant and meet people to allay fears and build community.

This exercise was especially beneficial because it provided culture-specific development suggestions—that is, ideas that worked in this unique organization. These weren't a bunch of textbook, generic recommendations. The executives began to see the power of learning from each other, giving and receiving feedback, and collaborating genuinely. Traditionally, when they came together for their quarterly leadership team meetings, the focus would be on information sharing—reporting what was happening in their units, asking and answering questions, and moving on. Rarely did they make real decisions as a group or even deliberate on the options—the meetings were more about presentation than discussion. But through this peer-coaching process, the participants began to see the power of teamwork.

As you can see, this one small module in the initial session built up all three areas the team needed to improve—CQ, EQ, and talent management. The executives increased their self-awareness by taking a deeper dive into their CQ/Change Intelligence Assessment results; they improved their social awareness by learning more about their peers; and they strengthened their self- and relationship-management ability by listening to suggestions from their peers. One leader said, "In my thirty-year career, I never saw an example of how a leader could be both strong and sensitive. I always thought empathy was a weakness. Now I know otherwise."

This strategy of combining CQ and EQ proved to be a winning one. The executives saw clearly that change needed to start with them, to move from the inside out. By achieving new insight into their EQ, they were able to see the impact of their leadership styles on their people—and, ultimately, on their business results. This led to a greater appreciation of how their CQ impacted their capacity to effectively and jointly manage change within their mills.

As the program cascaded down to the department-head level, to the executives' direct reports, each executive coached his or her own staff members. The vision of "leaders developing leaders" had become a reality. This empowered people with much-needed feedback from their managers, and began the process of transforming the culture to one of frequent conversations about professional development. In this way, leaders at all levels saw firsthand that, just as a lean culture depends on continuous improvement of its equipment and technical processes, so its people thrive in a climate of continuous development and feedback that hones their ability to intelligently adapt to change over time.

*   *   *

Let's now take a look at what we can learn from these case studies. First, what did these three organizations have in common?

- Each was undergoing major changes—mergers and acquisitions, the opportunity to transform their organization's approach to change management to obtain ROI for new technologies, the need to build a leadership pipeline.
- Each was undergoing several major changes at once.
- Each recognized the need for change to start at the top.
- Each executive team realized it needed to partner with leaders at all levels to bring the change to life.
- Each appreciated that the change had to be cascaded across the organizations' various departments and locations.

Now, what results did each organization obtain from the CQ System?

- They embedded a simple, powerful, versatile model for leading change.
- They learned a common approach to change, including a common language to talk about it.
- Seasoned leaders developed new leaders, to everyone's benefit.
- They achieved greater understanding, alignment, and engagement by consistently and proactively connecting with Hearts, Heads, and Hands.
- They reduced confusion, fear, and skepticism.

The three firms in these case studies were successful in increasing their CQ for several reasons:

- They started at the top.
- They adapted the way they changed.
- They instituted a consistent mindset and approach (the CQ System).
- They trained and coached leaders at all levels in the CQ model and tools.
- They engaged people's Hearts, Heads, and Hands throughout the change process.
- They actively solicited feedback through a variety of mechanisms and viewed resistance not as a problem in itself but as a sign of a larger issue that needed attention.

These factors are interconnected and mutually reinforcing. Starting at the top enabled executives to coach those below. Coaching sessions across levels enabled executives to hear direct feedback and avoid the isolation that so often accompanies distance from the front lines. And, crucially, the approach wasn't a one-time thing but an ongoing process. Indeed, it's often the follow-up that makes the endeavor take root: David Rock and Jeffrey Schwartz's article "The Neuroscience of Leadership" states that "a training program alone increased productivity 28 percent, but the addition of follow-up coaching to the training increased productivity 88 percent . . . many small bites of learning, digested over time, may be more efficient than large blocks of time spent in workshops. The key is getting people to pay sufficient attention to new ideas."[27]

A common language increases the probability that everyone is on the same page, and a common understanding of blind spots fosters less-defensive conversations about how to improve strategies and tactics. When organizational leaders discussed the causes of resistance, they unearthed opportunities to remove barriers that stood in the way of change-consistent behavior (Hands), clear communication about the business rationale for the change (Head), and a compelling case for why people should care (Heart).

In this way, building CQ drives a virtuous cycle that replaces the tiring treadmill of failed change projects and their byproducts: cynicism, damaged relationships, and loss of trust.

Tips for Using CQ in Your Organization

To put the CQ System to work in your company and enhance its ability to lead change, you need to

- Start at the top.
- Develop change leaders at all levels. Provide formal training as well as manager and peer coaching.
- Cascade down and move across the organization. Plant many seeds.
- Utilize the CQ methods and tools to develop a consistent language and approach to change.

- Integrate other change methodologies to develop a system-wide change toolkit.
- Avoid labeling initiatives as "programs." Change is constant and ubiquitous. Treat change like a way of life, which it is.
- Practice courageous conversations. As Ken Blanchard and Spencer Johnson remind us in their book *The One Minute Manager*, "Feedback is the breakfast of champions."[28] Get feedback and feedforward, from above and below.

If you regularly revisit these strategies and apply them in your organization, you'll soon begin to see the benefits of the CQ System across the company: change happens with less resistance and strife, becomes part of the organization's essence (rather than evaporating after a short period of time and leaving you short on results), and leads to positive outcomes at every level.

 Visit www.ChangeCatalysts.com/BookResources for a description of the change culture typically fostered by organizations with various CQ styles, and how leaders can capitalize on their culture's strengths and avoid its potential pitfalls.

CHAPTER 14

CQ AND THE STAGES OF THE CHANGE LIFECYCLE

In this chapter, we'll link CQ to the larger body of knowledge about organizational change. We've laid a solid foundation for what CQ is and explored a multitude of case studies depicting how building CQ benefits individuals, teams, and organizations. Now, we will explore how CQ can be deployed during the various stages of the change lifecycle on a practical level. To complement this discussion, we'll also discuss useful methods and tools from the disciplines of change management, strategic planning, and leadership development.

Before we go any further, let's draw a distinction between change leadership and change management that will help you understand how to apply the tools presented in this chapter. CQ is about diagnosing and developing your capacity to lead change—in other words, it's about change leadership. Change management, on the other hand, is a set of techniques that you, the change leader, can apply to a change process. As change leaders, we pick and choose the change management approaches and techniques to bring to bear on a change situation. CQ will help you as a change leader identify which change management tools you tend to gravitate toward based on your style—and which you may tend to overuse or, conversely, overlook.

The Change Lifecycle

From the early 1900s when Kurt Lewin introduced his unfreezing-moving-refreezing description of the change process, many models have been offered to help us understand the change lifecycle. Most are variations on a similar theme. To illustrate how to apply CQ during the change lifecycle, we'll use one of the more simple, straightforward models (see Figure 14.1), much like the one used by Kate Nelson and Stacy Aaron in *The Change Management Pocket Guide*[29]:

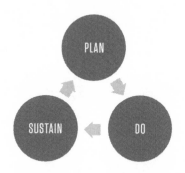

Figure 14.1: The Stages of the Change Lifecycle.

First you plan, then you do, then you sustain. Then, you start planning the next change. This table lists the major activities that occur at each stage in the change lifecycle.

Plan	Do	Sustain
• Create vision • Determine readiness • Craft plan	• Communicate • Train • Modify processes	• Adapt systems • Ensure integration • Examine lessons learned

Change leaders with different CQ profiles will experience different challenges and evince different strengths in each stage of the change lifecycle, and we'll look at those dynamics in the following pages. The purpose of this discussion is not to provide an exhaustive list of each type's challenges and strengths in the cycle, but rather to give you a representative sampling, along with associated recommendations and examples. To bring the discussion to life, I'll offer examples of how various tools were used at various stages by the three organizations introduced in the last chapter.

The Planning Stage

HEART-ORIENTED CHANGE LEADERS
(COACHES AND SOME CHAMPIONS, FACILITATORS, AND
ADAPTERS) IN THE PLANNING STAGE

Heart-oriented change leaders need to stay focused on strategy and tactics to facilitate a successful planning stage. They may find an **emphasis on project planning** particularly helpful.

For example, the Heart-heavy clinical leaders at the healthcare system resisted putting systems into place that they perceived as bureaucratic; they felt these would take time away from patient care. However, this mindset prevented them from developing a sound plan for the full-asset merger.

Once they realized this, they were able to leverage their director of finance, a Driver, to craft and own a detailed project plan, part of which each member of the leadership team had accountability to execute.

Heart-Oriented Change Leaders in the Planning Stage

You are good at . . .
• Taking the needs of a wide variety of stakeholders into account to assess the impact of a change and incorporate disparate needs into the plan • Reminding the change team to pay attention to its own development and team dynamics
But sometimes you . . .
• May not be as savvy in analyzing the viability of the change vision • May not create as detailed and explicit a change charter and plan as is ideal

HEAD-ORIENTED CHANGE LEADERS (VISIONARIES AND SOME DRIVERS, CHAMPIONS, AND ADAPTERS) IN THE PLANNING STAGE

Head-oriented change leaders need to keep people and process on their radar screen to facilitate a successful planning stage. **Stakeholder analysis** and a **leadership involvement plan** may be especially helpful for them.

For example, the Head-heavy leadership team at the steel mill had the vision of building up its leadership pipeline. Through discussions, they came to see two things: that they needed to develop their leadership skills and that they needed to be accountable for developing leaders below them.

Utilizing a stakeholder analysis and a leadership involvement plan helped them lay out a process to cascade leadership skills down the ranks and to enable others to be jointly accountable for execution of the plan.

Head-Oriented Change Leaders in the Planning Stage

You are good at...
• Creating compelling visions and business cases for change • Specifying goals for the change and laying the strategy to achieve them
But sometimes you...
• May neglect to secure advocates to sponsor the change • May not consider the impacts of the change on key stakeholders

HANDS-ORIENTED CHANGE LEADERS (EXECUTERS AND SOME FACILITATORS, DRIVERS, AND ADAPTERS) IN THE PLANNING STAGE

Hands-oriented change leaders need to keep stakeholders and goals on their radar screen to facilitate a successful planning stage. **Leadership alignment tools** can help them to that end.

For example, the Hands-heavy leadership team at the retail company crafted a very detailed plan to create and manage the HIT program. However, initially they created their plans in a vacuum, neglecting to vet their decisions by the firm's executive committee. When certain members of the executive team balked upon learning of some of the team's ideas, the team realized it needed to deploy a more intentional and proactive approach.

They used a leadership alignment process to guide their efforts and ensure the executives were aware of and supportive of their evolving tactics.

Hands-Oriented Change Leaders in the Planning Stage

You're good at . . .
<ul><li>Crafting a detailed project plan to execute the change</li><li>Being cognizant of the need to understand the future state, analyze the current state, and determine specific tactics to close the gap</li></ul>
But sometimes you . . .
<ul><li>May neglect to consider the impact and needs of all key stakeholders</li><li>May neglect to ask basic questions about the viability of the change from a business and people perspective</li></ul>

The Doing Stage

HEART-ORIENTED CHANGE LEADERS
(COACHES AND SOME CHAMPIONS, FACILITATORS,
AND ADAPTERS) IN THE DOING STAGE

Heart-led change leaders need to keep strategy and tactics on their radar screen to facilitate a successful Doing stage. **Implementation checklists** are a great way to help them do so.

For example, the Heart-led leadership team at the hospital recognized the need to craft a project plan during the Planning stage, but once implementation started, they realized that key activities were falling through the cracks. The team deployed an implementation checklist to guide their efforts as well as the activities of their direct reports, who were charged with executing many of the plan's tactical details. Doing so provided greater clarity and fostered alignment between team members and down into each of their organizations.

Heart-Oriented Change Leaders in the Doing Stage

You are good at ...

- Communicating about the change to foster awareness and understanding
- Encouraging involvement and providing positive feedback to keep people motivated as they "do" the change

But sometimes you ...

- May not keep a detailed focus on managing the project plan and ensuring all activities are occurring on time and meeting expectations
- May not be comfortable confronting leaders and other key stakeholders who are not living up to their commitments to the change

---

HEAD-ORIENTED CHANGE LEADERS (VISIONARIES AND SOME DRIVERS, CHAMPIONS, AND ADAPTERS) IN THE DOING STAGE

Head-oriented change leaders need to keep people and process on their radar screen to facilitate a successful Doing stage, and **feedback processes** can help them do this.

For example, the Head-heavy leadership team at the steel mill recognized during the Planning stage that it needed leaders to effectively transmit messages down through the ranks. However, during the Doing stage, they saw that they were in fact not receiving much "upward feedback" about how the changes were being received. The leadership team realized it needed to install structured feedback processes, just as it had installed coaching processes before.

Head-Oriented Change Leaders in the Doing Stage

You are good at . . .

- Keeping the organization moving toward the new vision
- Promoting the goal and progress achieved

But sometimes you . . .

- May not pay attention to or recognize the impact of changes on the organizational culture
- May neglect to consistently communicate with key stakeholders during the transition process

HANDS-ORIENTED CHANGE LEADERS (EXECUTERS AND SOME FACILITATORS, DRIVERS, AND ADAPTERS) IN THE DOING STAGE

Hands-oriented change leaders need to keep the stakeholders and goals on their radar screen to facilitate a successful Doing stage. **Readiness and impact assessments** can be especially useful here.

For example, during the Doing stage of its change initiative, the Hands-heavy team at the retail company learned that it needed to proactively engage managers at the various locations where HIT program participants would be stationed. Since this was a new program, managers weren't used to the idea of having a short-term, high-potential leader on staff. The team recognized the need to conduct a readiness assessment so they could better equip the managers for their new roles, and an impact assessment to understand how an influx of program participants and their unique needs would affect the receiving business units. In this way, they were able to target training materials for the managers and establish processes to mitigate any negative impact on the business.

Hands-Oriented Change Leaders in the Doing Stage

You are good at . . .
• Executing the project plan • Ensuring that stakeholders have the information, training, and tools to act consistently with the change
But sometimes you . . .
• May not be as apt to collect input on the impact of the changes on people and groups, or about how people are perceiving the change • May not be as cognizant of the bigger picture or the broader impact of the change on the business

The Sustaining Stage

HEART-ORIENTED CHANGE LEADERS
(COACHES AND SOME CHAMPIONS, FACILITATORS,
AND ADAPTERS) IN THE SUSTAINING STAGE

Heart-oriented change leaders need to keep strategy and tactics on their radar screen to facilitate a successful Sustaining stage. To help them do so, they can employ a **systems and structure action plan.**

For example, it became apparent to the hospital's Heart-heavy leadership team that the manager of the pharmacy department in the acquired hospital was not following certain protocols that had been established in the merger. Instead of sidelining this manager, the leadership team capitalized on its strengths in involving others and invited him to participate in crafting a systems and structure action plan for the merged healthcare system. Through participating in that process, he came to understand the rationale behind the protocols. Once that happened, he got on board to integrate the changes into his work process and reap the benefits of the improvement—along with the rest of the hospital.

Heart-Oriented Change Leaders in the Sustaining Stage

You are good at . . .
<ul><li>Staying cognizant of the need to align human resource systems with the change</li><li>Redefining organizational structures and individual roles and responsibilities to be consistent with the change</li></ul>
But sometimes you . . .
<ul><li>May not be as likely to define metrics to continually measure change outcomes over time</li><li>May not be as apt to initiate crucial conversations with leaders in parts of the organization that are not aligned with change processes and goals</li></ul>

HEAD-ORIENTED CHANGE LEADERS
(VISIONARIES AND SOME DRIVERS, CHAMPIONS,
AND ADAPTERS) IN THE SUSTAINING STAGE

Head-oriented change leaders have to focus on the people and the process to facilitate a successful Sustaining stage, and **knowledge-sharing mechanisms** can help them do so.

For example, the Head-heavy steel mill succeeded in improving its leadership pipeline through the developmental recommendations made by leaders to leaders. The suggestions they shared were proven and organization specific. To capture this wealth of knowledge, the leadership team deployed several knowledge-sharing mechanisms, including setting the expectation that ideas be written down when they arose in coaching conversations; that facilitators solicit ideas during the group training sessions; and that executives work with their external coaches to tease out the pivotal lessons they'd learned over the course of their careers.

Head-Oriented Change Leaders in the Sustaining Stage

You are good at . . .
• Highlighting improvements to the bottom line and organizational effectiveness resulting from the change process   • Recognizing the need for all the parts of the system to work together to sustain the change, and advocating for this alignment
But sometimes you . . .
• May neglect or delegate and not keep a firm handle on the details of the change-integration process   • May be tempted to dive into more change before the current changes are fully institutionalized and before the organization is ready

HANDS-ORIENTED CHANGE LEADERS (EXECUTERS AND SOME FACILITATORS, DRIVERS, AND ADAPTERS) IN THE SUSTAINING STAGE

Hands-oriented change leaders need to keep the various stakeholders and goals of a change project at the top of their mind during the Sustaining stage. **Human resource systems alignment tools** can help them achieve that end.

For example, even after managers at the various locations where HIT program participants were stationed were trained and given other support materials for how to work with these high-potential leaders, there was still variability in the managers' performances. Through conducting an HR systems alignment audit, the program's leadership team realized that it needed to modify the performance-management system and incorporate the program's ultimate goals into each manager's objectives.

Hands-Oriented Change Leaders in the Sustaining Stage

You are good at . . .
• Delineating metrics and measurement processes to assess the impact and progress of the change • Creating effective plans to transition to steady-state operations
But sometimes you . . .
• May overlook the need to modify the organizational structure and individual roles to be consistent with the change • May assume people have adopted changes because they checked off activities on their plan, when they haven't actually implemented the change

*   *   *

Change leaders have a variety of tools at their disposal, any of which they can bring to bear during the various stages of the change lifecycle. If you stay mindful of the combination of your change leader style and the dynamics of the various stages, you'll be able to select the tools to help you meet critical change challenges, especially those you may be apt to overlook, downplay, or avoid.

 Visit www.ChangeCatalysts.com/BookResources for a table listing each Change Lifecycle Stage (Plan-Do-Sustain) and a deeper description of tools you can deploy for each change leader style.

CHAPTER 15

CQ AND THE PHASES OF HUMAN REACTIONS TO CHANGE

In the last chapter, you learned how you can deploy CQ during the various stages of the change lifecycle. In this chapter, you'll see how CQ can benefit change leaders as they endeavor to help others move through the phases of change reactions that people experience on a psychological level. Throughout the discussion, I'll recommend methods and tools from the disciplines of change management, strategic planning, and leadership development—tools that will help you shore up your blind spots and move the change process forward.

When people encounter change, they progress through a series of phases. There are several frameworks that help clarify human reaction to change, but the one you'll learn about in this chapter is adapted to CQ and based on the work of Elisabeth Kübler-Ross, who studied human reactions to death and dying. She discovered that not everyone, but many people, progressed through a similar set of thoughts, perceptions, and experiences. This model can be applied to understanding the human reaction to change, since most people initially perceive change as a threat, a danger—something to be feared.

Coping with change is a process that moves people from a focus on the past to a focus on the future, and from a focus on what's happening in their external environment to a focus on what's happening inside themselves. When they first learn of an impending change, particularly a significant one, many people go into *denial*. (See figure 15.1.) Next comes *resistance*, or at least what looks and feels like resistance to change leaders. If the resistance is effectively managed, people move to the *exploration* stage, testing the new direction. Finally, *commitment* occurs.

Figure 15.1: The Phases of Human Reactions to Change

Understanding these reactions to change can help you predict them and can help you deploy effective approaches to addressing them. Doing so is fundamental to your ability to lead through any major change project.

The Denial Phase

Denial is a normal psychological defense mechanism. And when it comes to organizational change, it's an understandable reaction, given the "program of the year" phenomenon and the discomfort that accompanies any major alteration in our work lives. Denial is a coping skill that enables us to protect ourselves. It helps us navigate all the new information we're constantly bombarded with in modern life.

As a leader, how do you know when your people are in the denial stage? You'll know when they say things like, "It's no big deal" or, "It won't affect us" or, "We'll outlive this new manager and the changes he's trying to make, just like the last guy corporate tried to shove down our throats." People may avoid you, the change leader, just as they may avoid any exposure to the change process. Some go into withdrawal, seeming to hide out. Others may appear numb, confused, or off balance.

Different change leader styles will have different strengths in helping people through the denial stage. They also have different blind spots, and there are tools that can help them more effectively lead others through this challenging time at the onset of a change initiative.

HEART-ORIENTED CHANGE LEADERS (COACHES AND SOME CHAMPIONS, FACILITATORS, AND ADAPTERS) IN THE DENIAL PHASE

Heart-oriented change leaders are the most sensitive to the emotions other people experience in the denial phase. They're usually uncomfortable with making others uncomfortable—but moving out of one's comfort zone is essential to getting out of denial.

- To leverage your strengths: Use your natural inquisitiveness about people to understand their level of awareness of the change, and use your winning humor and informal style to take an adventurous attitude toward the change as you explain how it might affect individuals and groups.
- To overcome a potential blind spot: Try visual management. If "seeing is believing," the more visual cues you give people about the

change, the more they'll begin to believe it is really happening. Try things like posters, scorecards, and dashboards.

HEAD-ORIENTED CHANGE LEADERS (VISIONARIES AND SOME DRIVERS, CHAMPIONS, AND ADAPTERS) IN THE DENIAL PHASE

Head-driven change leaders can be so caught up in getting on with the change that they may fail to perceive any denial at all in others. Eventually, they may look around and ask themselves, "Where is everyone?" For these change leaders, there are two big challenges during the denial stage: first, recognizing that it is occurring, and second, taking the time to deal with it effectively.

- To leverage your strengths: Formally announce the change. It's surprising how often this seemingly simple act is neglected or carried out in a way that causes confusion and uncertainty. Provide as much information as you can about change goals—the *why* and the *what*. Likewise, redirect attention toward the change. Have candid conversations with people about why the old way no longer works and how the new way benefits everyone. Give compelling, vivid data and plenty of examples.

- To overcome a potential blind spot: Try storytelling in the context of two-way meetings (one-on-one and in groups). This may come naturally to Champions, but for many Visionaries and most Drivers this may be a stretch. Nevertheless, as the most strategic and forward looking of the change leaders, help paint a picture for others about where the change is going to take the organization. Telling stories from a personal perspective allows people to relate to you as a change leader and encourages them to come to you with questions and concerns through all the change phases.

HANDS-ORIENTED CHANGE LEADERS
(EXECUTERS AND SOME FACILITATORS, DRIVERS, AND
ADAPTERS) IN THE DENIAL PHASE

Similar to Head-driven change leaders, Hands-driven change leaders may not notice signs of denial. They can be so focused on assigning responsibilities for specific tasks that they fail to see that these tasks aren't being carried out at all (or are being carried out in a lackluster manner). Hands-oriented change leaders may be good at managing project groups and sharing information with those below them, but they may not consistently engage in the dialogue that would help them understand people's perceptions and reactions.

- To leverage a strength: Let people know what to expect, and clarify any areas of ambiguity. Since Hands-heavy change leaders often have a firm handle on the project plan, provide as much information as you can about process, timing, and deliverables at the onset. This will set expectations and quell concerns.

- To overcome a potential blind spot: Work to build a cohesive team. There are a variety of team-building techniques that help create a climate of open sharing. By facilitating these sessions with their project team and other groups impacted by the change, Hands-oriented change leaders can learn to genuinely listen to and appreciate where people are coming from. This allows them to unearth and address denial and its various manifestations.

The Resistance Phase

In physics, *resistance* is defined as "a force that tends to oppose or retard motion." During the resistance stage, it can appear that people are actively working in opposition to the change. However, in biology, *resistance* is defined as "the capacity of an organism to protect itself from harm." One of the core themes of the CQ System is that what often seems to be resistance in others is really a symptom of us as change leaders not giving people what they need to "get" it, "want" it, or "do" it.

As a leader, how do you know when your people are in the Resistance stage? Resistance can take many forms, but it usually doesn't require a doctorate in psychology to pick up on even subtle forms of opposition to the change. In the Resistance stage, participation is the most variable. Some become angry, and conflicts may abound. Others withdraw and seem helpless. People may grieve for what they fear will be lost—whether it's security, status, skills, or social relationships. Some may become passive-aggressive, seeming to comply but then quietly resisting. Others may engage in overt sabotage.

Different change leader styles display different strengths as they help people through the Resistance stage. They also have their own blind spots, but there are tools that can help them more effectively lead at this challenging time in a change initiative. During the Resistance stage, employing lessons and tools from Emotional Intelligence (EQ) can be invaluable.

HEART-ORIENTED CHANGE LEADERS
(COACHES AND SOME CHAMPIONS, FACILITATORS, AND
ADAPTERS) IN THE RESISTANCE PHASE

Heart-led change leaders are especially adept at using their communication skills to surface, honor, and explore resistance. But, particularly if they are out in front as the "face" of the change, Heart-oriented leaders may be prone to take resistance personally. This may lead to the change leader becoming demoralized him- or herself.

- To leverage your strengths: Communicate early and optimistically. Freely discuss changes to prevent—or at least mitigate—rumors.

- To overcome a potential blind spot: Build your confidence in managing conflict and overcome the tendency to deflect or downplay signs of resistance. Moreover, resist the temptation to make people feel guilty, disloyal, or somehow wrong for expressing it. Instead, don't take resistance personally, and deal with it head-on.

HEAD-ORIENTED CHANGE LEADERS (VISIONARIES AND SOME DRIVERS, CHAMPIONS, AND ADAPTERS) IN THE RESISTANCE PHASE

Because they are so intent on moving toward the new vision—preferably quickly—Head-driven change leaders can become extremely frustrated with others during the Resistance stage. They are the most likely to be tempted to "overcome" resistance by resorting to threats, coercion, or forms of bribery. These change leaders must learn that sometimes one must go slow to go fast. Dealing proactively and positively with resistance can provide an excellent source of input—the change leader can identify potential derailers, time wasters, and other issues that might inhibit the change plan.

- To leverage your strengths: Create rituals to help people say goodbye to the old way. Of all the change leader styles, you are the most focused on moving forward to the new and different, so mark the passage away from the old. Create tangible and symbolic ways to retire former systems, processes, and tools to pave the way for the new.

- To overcome a potential blind spot: Use your EQ to listen actively and empathetically. Hold forums to help yourself understand sources of resistance. Once people express themselves, acknowledge their feelings, respond with feeling, and don't try to talk people out of their emotions.

HANDS-ORIENTED CHANGE LEADERS
(EXECUTERS AND SOME FACILITATORS, DRIVERS, AND
ADAPTERS) IN THE RESISTANCE PHASE

Hands-led change leaders may react to resistance by holding themselves and their teams to the grindstone, doggedly adhering to the project plan and cracking down on the noncompliant. But basic compliance isn't the same as commitment, and it can morph into a malicious form of compliance or passive-aggressiveness. Moreover, Hands-led change leaders can neglect the perceptions of those who will ultimately be impacted by the change even though they don't have specific roles on the project plan.

- To leverage a strength: Use your skills in managing accountabilities to gently point out when individuals aren't living up to their responsibilities. Appreciate these instances as potential symptoms of a deeper issue with the change. Avoid discounting what you see or considering it unimportant. Instead, objectively and nondefensively explore the person's reasons for veering off track, and be open to hearing new information. Armed with this data, facilitate new agreements to get the person back in alignment.

- To overcome a potential blind spot: Create ownership of the change. Leverage your strength in assigning accountabilities, but this time stretch yourself and cast a wider net for additional individuals and groups to involve. Assign accountabilities for specific tasks to people in different levels and teams (as long as their involvement makes sense); this can provide you with more sources of feedback and reveal important reactions and barriers. Moreover, participation is one of the most effective means to promote understanding and, ultimately, commitment.

The Exploration Phase

After the pain of the Resistance stage, the Exploration stage can feel like a welcome relief. Finally, people transition from working against the change to moving toward it. You hear people say things like, "Let's try it!" Some cautiously stick their big toe in the water, while others jump right into the deep end.

Regardless of their pace of exploration, people finally seem to understand the change and display a more positive attitude toward it. Acceptance increases. Instead of feeling controlled, people experience a sense of autonomy. They begin to experiment with the change, look for creative alternatives, and unleash fresh energy.

Yet, unleashing energy can lead to challenging dynamics in the Exploration stage. People are still testing—they are still novices with respect to the new way of doing things. That can result in a period of chaos and confusion. People craft an abundance of ideas, but the very abundance can overwhelm them.

Different change leader styles display different strengths as they manage the energy of the Exploration stage. They also have different blind spots, and there are tools that can help them more effectively lead their people through this exciting phase.

HEART-ORIENTED CHANGE LEADERS
(COACHES AND SOME CHAMPIONS, FACILITATORS,
AND ADAPTERS) IN THE EXPLORATION PHASE

Heart-led change leaders resonate with the positive emotional energy of the Exploration stage. As leaders, they can also use this stage to build muscle in facilitating their teams to gather data and make decisions in a structured manner.

- To leverage your strengths: Avidly promote teamwork. Emphasize the key stakeholders' mutual responsibility for the change and for each other. During the Exploration stage, people often forge powerful bonds, particularly if they were able to successfully navigate divisive conflicts during the Resistance stage.

- To overcome a potential blind spot: Develop your capacity to harness the voluminous amount of ideas being brought forth. Although they are typically done at the onset of a change process, SWOT (Strengths-Weaknesses-Opportunities-Threats) Analyses can help you appreciate people's evolving perceptions of the change, which can then be incorporated into strategies and plans.

HEAD-ORIENTED CHANGE LEADERS (VISIONARIES AND SOME DRIVERS, CHAMPIONS, AND ADAPTERS) IN THE EXPLORATION PHASE

Head-oriented change leaders tend to be relieved during the exploration stage to "finally" see momentum for enacting their vision. The Exploration phase is an excellent time to engage people in "getting real" about objectives, and a perfect opportunity for Head-driven change leaders to get in the trenches with their people.

- To leverage your strengths: Encourage people to concentrate on the right priorities. It has been said that leadership is the art of focusing people's attention. With all the ideas and options under consideration, channel people's energy in appropriate directions.

- To overcome a potential blind spot: Work with people to help them translate system-wide and long-range change visions into measurable, group-specific objectives. Encouraging people to set their own success goals fosters independence and personal responsibility. People own what they help create.

HANDS-ORIENTED CHANGE LEADERS
(EXECUTERS AND SOME FACILITATORS, DRIVERS, AND
ADAPTERS) IN THE EXPLORATION PHASE

Hands-heavy change leaders are pleased to see the first signs of implementation begin during the exploration stage. The task of managing the project plan suddenly begins to feel less onerous, less like pushing on string.

- To leverage your strengths: Provide training and tools. Hands-oriented change leaders are the most likely to understand what people need at ground level to behave consistently with the change. At the exploration stage, people will be open to, if not thirsty for, anything that enables them to adapt to the new way of life.

- To overcome a potential blind spot: Offer people the opportunity to engage in creative problem solving using techniques like brainstorming, force-field analysis, and gap analysis. Hands-oriented change leaders can get married to their plan and neglect to step back and ask fundamental questions about whether the planned way is still the right way. Get people's creative juices flowing during the exploration stage—it can yield fresh approaches to nagging problems. Allow others to research, evaluate, and make recommendations for every aspect of the change process.

The Commitment Phase

The Commitment phase is the Holy Grail of any change initiative. Now people are "on board" and have "bought in," and groups are "aligned" and "integrated." People support the change through their words and their actions. Behaviors are in sync with long-range change goals, and short-term objectives that aren't consistent with change are subordinated. Management actively invests resources to sustain the change. Cooperation and teamwork abound. People say, "We did it!" and experience the satisfaction that comes with accomplishing a challenging goal.

However, the change leader's role isn't over. In the Commitment phase, change leaders can deploy a variety of tactics to sustain the change and keep people moving forward.

HEART-ORIENTED CHANGE LEADERS (COACHES AND SOME CHAMPIONS, FACILITATORS, AND ADAPTERS) IN THE COMMITMENT PHASE

Heart-led change leaders adore the camaraderie that often accompanies the Commitment phase. As leaders, they can also use this stage to build muscle in designing systems to support people in sustaining the change.

- To leverage your strengths: Celebrate successes. Reward individuals and teams who have played key roles in the change process. In communications, highlight the new things people are doing that are contributing to success so others can emulate them.

- To overcome a potential blind spot: Remember to put systems and processes in place to sustain the change. Work with people and teams to install wedges that prevent backsliding. Try approaches from the continuous improvement toolkit. Transfer ownership of new procedures to those who will eventually be responsible for them. Strive to empower, not to create dependence.

HEAD-ORIENTED CHANGE LEADERS (VISIONARIES AND SOME DRIVERS, CHAMPIONS, AND ADAPTERS) IN THE COMMITMENT PHASE

Head-oriented change leaders take great pride in seeing their vision become a reality. But they need to remember to make sure the change is truly sustained prior to launching into the next new program.

- To leverage your strengths: Partner with fellow leaders to ensure that priorities are aligned with the change, on both strategic and tactical levels. Determine appropriate metrics to measure and manage over time.
- To overcome a potential blind spot: Continue to invest your time and resources into making sure the changes stick. Pay attention to cultural dynamics: they may alert you to risks before they become full-fledged issues. Consider an engagement survey or another tool to solicit feedback over time.

HANDS-ORIENTED CHANGE LEADERS (EXECUTERS AND SOME FACILITATORS, DRIVERS, AND ADAPTERS) IN THE COMMITMENT PHASE

Hands-driven change leaders experience a sense of accomplishment during the commitment phase as they see people coming together to work the plan. But these change leaders need to be on guard. They can't assume that because the plan is accomplished and boxes are checked that their role as leaders is complete.

- To leverage your strengths: Extend the project plan beyond where it would normally end, and delineate mechanisms to help people monitor the change's progress over time. Involve people in crafting and managing those mechanisms.
- To overcome a potential blind spot: Facilitate a "lessons learned" session or a series of focus groups. This will help you fully understand people's perceptions of the change and the impact it's had on them. Understand that people and groups may still have to fully transition to the new way of working. Provide resources to help them do so, and continue the two-way feedback process.

*   *   *

Teams and organizations, like individuals, also go through similar stages. Collections of people often pass through the denial, resistance, exploration, and commitment phases in sync. As change leaders, it's essential that we diagnose and deal with these dynamics at the team and organizational level as well.

And, particularly during significant changes, or when multiple changes are occurring at once, progress through the phases may not be linear. Instead, people may move from denial, to resistance, and then back to denial because they just can't believe that yet another change is happening. They might say, "See! They switched gears again. Nothing will really change. It's business as usual."

It's frighteningly easy for people to revert to the denial phase, or to stay stuck in resistance, and that's one reason why it's so critical for change leaders to be armed with a knowledge of CQ and all the supplementary models and methods covered in the last two chapters. The more tools in your toolkit, the better equipped you are to give people what they need and to help everyone—including yourself—get where they want to go.

 Visit www.ChangeCatalysts.com/BookResources for a table listing each phase of human reactions to change (Denial-Resistance-Exploration-Commitment) and a more detailed list of coaching suggestions for each change leader style.

CHAPTER 16

BRINGING IT ALL TOGETHER

So many of today's leaders are at best apprehensive and at worst terrified by the prospect of looming change in their organization, team, or career. I began this book by asking:

- Is your organization struggling in the current economy, forced to make tough business decisions that no one wants to make?
- Are you tired of the "program of the year," and do you want to know how to make change stick?
- Are you frustrated by your inability to overcome resistance to new ways of working?

By this point, I hope you've derived insights that will help you lead the many changes you're bombarded with—and do so with greater skill and ease. With the power of CQ in your grasp, you'll find that you lead in a way that garners you more satisfaction, encourages fruitful collaboration from your team, and gives you a better chance of generating significant return on investment for your organization.

Here's the bottom line of this book: When people talk about change, they often fixate on the need to "overcome resistance." That puts the focus squarely on others—as if it's the leader's job to do something *to* or *in spite of* someone else. But it's not others that stand between you and leading positive, pervasive change. We must understand and change ourselves first; only then can we lead others to change.

Actually, to correct myself, a subtle distinction: it's not about changing ourselves, it's about changing our behaviors. It's about adapting our styles, not fundamentally changing who we are. It's about remaining true to ourselves so we can become more effective as leaders. Change starts with awareness, moves to acceptance, and then continues to adaptation and action. That's the intent of this book—to help you become aware of your change leadership style, to help you accept your strengths and weaknesses, to build your power to adapt your behaviors, and to spur you on to the actions that will catalyze powerful change in your career, team, and organization.

As you build awareness—and strengthen your Heart, Head, and Hands—you'll get better at selecting the right tools for the right situation, and you'll bolster your effectiveness as a change leader each time you do. And when CQ is integrated at the team and organizational levels—and complemented by tools that address the change lifecycle and psychological reactions to change—the probability of successful, sustainable change increases dramatically.

In these times of tremendous change—economic, political, demographic, and cultural, on both the local and global levels—CQ is crucial for realizing a new and better future for ourselves, our workplaces, and our world.

WEBSITE RESOURCES

To keep building your change intelligence, visit www.ChangeCatalysts.com, where you can sign up for a newsletter that regularly gives you fresh tips. Here is a list of Change Intelligent information you can access via the website right away, to deepen and extend your CQ learning journey:

- Video of a keynote speech about CQ.
- Downloadable case studies about how individuals, teams, and organizations built their CQ and the results they achieved.
- Downloadable brochure and details about the CQ/Change Intelligence Certification Program, approved for credit by the Association of Change Management Professionals (ACMP), Association for Talent Development (ATD), Human Resources Certification Institute (HRCI), International Coach Federation (ICF), Project Management Institute (PMI), and Society for Human Resource Management (SHRM).
- Downloadable white papers containing actionable research results from the global CQ/Change Intelligence Assessment database.
- Blog posts and newsletter articles for you, free CQ Tools, and two free chapters of this book that you can share with colleagues.
- Downloadable brochure and link to Change Intelligent eLearning courses, with versions for People Leaders and Team Members, available for your own self-study as well as to bring CQ to your organization in an online, scalable, globally accessible format.

In addition, by visiting **www.ChangeCatalysts.com/BookResources** you'll have access to the following resources mentioned throughout this book (Remember that you cannot navigate to the Book

Resources page directly from the main www.ChangeCatalysts.com website; you need to type the URL exactly as it is written here—**www.ChangeCatalysts.com/BookResources**—because it is a "hidden" page available only to book buyers.):

- A reading list that will help you further explore the topics mentioned in chapter 1, including change management theory and models, change management assessments and tools, relevant neuroscience research, and the concept of multiple intelligences.

- A reading list to help you deal with the unique dynamics faced by leaders at the supervisory, project management, and executive levels (Chapter 2).

- The CQ/Change Intelligence˚ Triangle Graphic as well as more information about the CQ/Change Intelligence˚ Assessment, including a downloadable description and information about how to access it to learn your Change Leader Style and obtain customized developmental recommendations (Chapter 3).

- Additional coaching hints on how Coaches can leverage their strengths and shore up their blind spots (Chapter 4).

- Additional coaching hints on how Visionaries can leverage their strengths and shore up their blind spots (Chapter 5).

- Additional coaching hints on how Executers can leverage their strengths and shore up their blind spots (Chapter 6).

- Additional coaching hints on how Champions can leverage their strengths and shore up their blind spots (Chapter 7).

- Additional coaching hints on how Drivers can leverage their strengths and shore up their blind spots (Chapter 8).

- Additional coaching hints on how Facilitators can leverage their strengths and shore up their blind spots (Chapter 9).

- Additional coaching hints on how Adapters can leverage their strengths and shore up their blind spots (Chapter 10).
- Tips for facilitating an initial CQ®-based session and how to handle common participant questions (Chapter 12).
- A description of the change culture typically fostered by organizations with various CQ styles, and how leaders can capitalize on their culture's strengths and avoid its potential pitfalls (Chapter 13).
- A table listing each Change Lifecycle Stage (Plan-Do-Sustain) and a deeper description of tools you can deploy for each change leader style (Chapter 14).
- A table listing each phase of the human reaction to change (Denial-Resistance-Exploration-Commitment) and a more detailed list of coaching suggestions for each change leader style (Chapter 15).

ACKNOWLEDGMENTS

I wish to thank all my clients over the years, who taught me so much about leading change. In particular, thank you to the individuals who participated in the CQ pilot test and the organizations that graciously gave me access for the CQ beta test. I am grateful to Tom Sawyer and Ray Grymski for their assistance in securing beta test sites.

Thanks to Clarence Trowbridge for being my faithful friend and steadfast colleague.

Thanks to Sam Horn, my first coach in the writing and publishing business.

Thanks to Elizabeth Marshall, book strategist, who midwifed this work and shepherded me through this brave new world.

Thanks to my wonderful team at the Greenleaf Book Group, from project management to marketing to distribution, with special appreciation to my concept editor Bill Crawford and substantive editor Aaron Hierholzer.

And finally, most importantly, thanks to my husband, Mike; son, Eric; and daughter, Veronica, for all your love, patience, and unwavering encouragement and support.

REFERENCES

CHAPTER 1

1   David Rock and Jeffrey Schwartz, "The Neuroscience of Leadership," *Strategy+Business*, issue 43, Summer 2006, pp. 3, 5.

2   Rick Maurer, *Beyond the Wall of Resistance* (Austin, TX: Bard Press, 2010).

3   Capgemini Consulting and The Economist Intelligence Unit, "Trends in Business Transformation: Study of European Executives," April 2007, p. 5.

4   Michael Haid, "Changing How You Manage Change," *The Linkage Leader* newsletter, www.LinkageInc.com—reporting results of a Right Management poll of 427 human resource professionals conducted in March 2010 (results rounded to the nearest percent).

5   Rock and Schwartz, "The Neuroscience of Leadership," p. 3.

CHAPTER 4

6   Jim Collins, "Good to Great," *Fast Company*, October 2001, p. 4.

7   Jenna Goudreau, "America's Happiest Companies," Forbes.com, October 29, 2010.

8   Shawn Achor, *The Happiness Advantage: The Seven Principles of Positive Psychology That Fuel Success and Performance at Work* (New York: Crown Publishing, 2010).

9   Steve Coats, "Being Truly Led," http://www.leadershipchallenge.com/Leaders-Section-Articles-Stories-Detail/the-five-practices-being-truly-led.aspx.

10 Jim Asplund and Nikki Blacksmith, "The Secret of Higher Performance," *Gallup Business Journal*, p. 1, http://businessjournal.gallup.com/content/147383/Secret-Higher-Performance.aspx.

11 James M. Kouzes and Barry Z. Posner, *Encouraging the Heart* (San Francisco: Jossey-Bass, 2003), p. xvi.

CHAPTER 5

12 Joel Barker, "The Power of Vision" speech, http://www.joelbarker.com.

13 Tony Mayo, "The Importance of Vision," *HBR Blog*, October 29, 2007.

CHAPTER 6

14 Timothy D. Wilson, *Redirect: The Surprising New Science of Psychological Change*, 2011 (New York: Hachette Book Group, 2011), p. 68.

15 Larry Bossidy and Ram Charan, *Execution* (New York: Crown Publishing group, 2002).

16 Maurer, *Beyond the Wall of Resistance*, pp. 12–13.

CHAPTER 7

17 Rosabeth Moss Kanter, *Evolve!* (Boston: Harvard Business School Press, 2001), p. 258.

18 Jim Clemmer, "Nurturing Change Champions," *The Practical Leader* blog, http://www.clemmergroup.com/nurturing-change-champions.php.

CHAPTER 8

19 John P. Kotter, *The Heart of Change* (Boston: Harvard Business School Press, 2002), Contents.

20 Maurer, *Beyond the Wall of Resistance*, p. 13.

CHAPTER 9

21 Kotter, *The Heart of Change*, 2002, pp. 1–2.

CHAPTER 10

22 Kousez and Posner, *The Leadership Challenge*, p. viii.

23 Rock and Schwartz, "The Neuroscience of Leadership," p. 8.

CHAPTER 11

24 Marshall Goldsmith, *What Got You Here Won't Get You There* (New York: Hyperion, 2007), pp. 7, 13.

CHAPTER 13

25 Casey Ichniowski, Kathryn Shaw, and Giovanna Prennushi, "The Effects of Human Resource Management Practices on Productivity," *Mimeograph*, Columbia University, June 10, 1993.

26 Richard E. Boyatzis and Ellen Van Oosten, "Developing Emotionally Intelligent Organizations," *International Executive Development Programmes, 7th Edition,* ed. Roderick Millar (London: Kogan Page Publishers, 2002).

27 Rock and Schwartz, "The Neuroscience of Leadership," pp. 8–9.

28 Ken Blanchard and Spencer Johnson, *The One Minute Manager* (New York: William Morrow, 1982).

CHAPTER 14

29 Kate Nelson and Stacy Aaron, *The Change Management Pocket Guide* (Cincinnati, OH: Change Guides, 2005).

ABOUT THE AUTHOR

Barbara A. Trautlein, PhD, is a change leadership international speaker, author, consultant, and researcher with more than thirty years of experience empowering leaders to achieve transformational personal and professional goals.

Through her company, Change Catalysts, Barbara provides her expertise to all levels of leaders at Fortune 500 companies, in addition to small- and mid-sized businesses and non-profits. During her career, Barbara has guided major change initiatives spanning diverse industries undergoing massive disruption ranging from healthcare to high tech, refineries to retail, and manufacturing to government. She has coached, trained, and certified thousands of change leaders from CEOs to the front line.

Barbara and her team are known for "making it real in the field." Whether partnering with C-level executives in the board room or walking the shop floor with union workers at a steel mill, Barbara is able to share strategies and tactics that are accessible, actionable, and immediately applicable.

An internationally recognized expert, Barbara conducts global research on leadership and change management best practices. Her unique identity as a scientist-practitioner has made her an in-demand speaker at conferences around the world.

As a speaker and strategist, Barbara has consulted with many leading brands and organizations in industries experiencing significant disruption, including Abbott Laboratories, Ascension Healthcare, Blue Cross/Blue Shield, BP, Cisco, the National Institutes of Health, and Northwestern University. She holds a PhD in organizational psychology from the University of Michigan.

Made in the USA
Columbia, SC
23 May 2024

36107271R00164